IRON
HONEY
GOLD

Three lives hath one life—
Iron, honey, gold.
The gold, the honey gone—
Left is the hard and cold.
ISAAC ROSENBERG

IRON
HONEY
GOLD

AN ANTHOLOGY OF POEMS
COMPILED BY

DAVID HOLBROOK

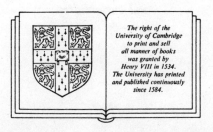

The right of the
University of Cambridge
to print and sell
all manner of books
was granted by
Henry VIII in 1534.
The University has printed
and published continuously
since 1584.

CAMBRIDGE UNIVERSITY PRESS

CAMBRIDGE
NEW YORK   NEW ROCHELLE
MELBOURNE   SYDNEY

Published by the Press Syndicate of the University of Cambridge
The Pitt Building, Trumpington Street, Cambridge CB2 1RP
32 East 57th Street, New York, NY 10022, USA
10 Stamford Road, Oakleigh, Melbourne 3166, Australia

Selection © Cambridge University Press 1961, 1965, 1988

First published 1961 as volume 1 of a 2 volume edition.
Second edition 1965 as volumes 1 and 2 of a 4 volume edition.
Third edition 1988.

Printed in Great Britain at the University Press, Cambridge

British Library cataloguing in publication data

Iron, honey, gold: an anthology – 3rd ed.
1. Poetry in English – Anthologies
I. Holbrook, David, *1923*–
821′.008

ISBN 0 521 36259 8

For
R.B.F., R.O'M. & D.T.
and our children

CONTENTS

v

vii

The Pedlar of Spells

LU YU

Translated by Arthur Waley

An old man selling charms in a cranny of the town wall;
He writes out spells to bless the silkworms and spells
                              to protect the corn.
With the money he gets each day he only buys wine;
But he does not worry when his legs get wobbly,
                              for he has a boy to lean on.

A Widow's Weeds

WALTER DE LA MARE

A poor old Widow in her weeds
Sowed her garden with wild-flower seeds;
Not too shallow, and not too deep,
And down came April drip-drip-drip.
Up shone May, like gold, and soon
Green as an arbour grew leafy June.
And now all summer she sits and sews
Where willow-herb, comfrey, bugloss blows,
Teasle and tansy, meadowsweet,
Campion, toadflax, and rough hawksbit;
Brown bee orchis, and Peals of Bells;
Clover, burnet, and thyme she smells;
Like Oberon's meadows her garden is
Drowsy from dawn till dusk with bees.
Weeps she never, but sometimes sighs,
And peeps at her garden with bright brown eyes;
A poor old Widow in her weeds.

I

Birds at Winter Nightfall

THOMAS HARDY

Triolet

Around the house the flakes fly faster,
And all the berries now are gone
From holly and cotonea-aster
Around the house. The flakes fly!—faster
Shutting indoors that crumb-outcaster
We used to see upon the lawn
Around the house. The flakes fly faster,
And all the berries now are gone!

As Adam Early in the Morning

WALT WHITMAN

As Adam early in the morning,
Walking forth from the bower refresh'd with sleep,
Behold me where I pass, hear my voice, approach,
Touch me, touch the palm of your hand to my body as I pass,
Be not afraid of my body.

The Derby Ram

ANONYMOUS

As I went down to Derby town,
'Twas on a market day,
And there I met the finest ram
Was ever fed on hay.
Riddle to my rye, riddle to my rye.

The wool upon this sheep's back
It grew up to the sky,
The eagles built their nests in it,
I heard the young ones cry.

The horns upon this ram's head
They grew up to the moon;
The preacher went up in April
And never was down till June.

The wool upon this sheep's tail
Was very fine and thin;
It took all the ladies in Derby town
Seven years to spin.

This ram he had four feet
And on them he did stand;
And every foot he had
Would cover an acre of land.

Every tooth this ram had
Was hollow as a horn;
They took one out and measured it,
It held a barrel of corn.

This ram's head was
As big as Noah's ark;
My dog ran up his nostrils,
And turned around and barked.

The one that killed this ram
Was up to his knees in blood;
And the one that held the basin
Was washed away in the flood.

3

It took all the men in Derby town
To haul away his horns;
And all the ladies in Derby town
To roll away his bones.

And if you don't believe me
And think it is a lie;
You go down to Derby town
And see as well as I.

As ye Came from the Holy Land

SIR WALTER RALEIGH

As ye came from the holy land
  Of Walsinghame,
Met you not with my true love
  By the way as you came?

How should I know your true love,
  That have met many a one,
As I came from the holy land,
  That have come, that have gone?

She is neither white nor brown,
  But as the heavens fair:
There is none hath her form divine
  In the earth or the air.

Such a one did I meet, good sir,
  Such an angelic face,
Who like a nymph, like a queen, did appear
  In her gait, in her grace.

She hath left me here alone
   All alone, as unknown,
Who sometime did me lead with herself,
   And me loved as her own.

What's the cause that she leaves you alone
   And a new way doth take,
That sometime did love you as her own,
   And her joy did you make?

I have loved her all my youth,
   But now am old, as you see:
Love likes not the falling fruit,
   Nor the witherèd tree.

Know that Love is a careless child,
   And forgets promise past:
He is blind, he is deaf when he list,
   And in faith never fast.

His desire is a dureless content,
   And a trustless joy;
He is won with a world of despair,
   And is lost with a toy.

Of womankind such indeed is the love,
   Or the word love abusèd,
Under which many childish desires
   And conceits are excusèd.

But true love is a durable fire,
   In the mind ever burning,
Never sick, never dead, never cold,
   From itself never turning.

The Shad

ANONYMOUS

Bait a hook to catch a shad,
The first thing he bit was my old Dad.
Pulled her away with all my might,
Trying for to get the old man out.
Fish-pole broke and I got mad,
Down to the bottom went old Dad.

Thunder

WALTER DE LA MARE

Call the cows home!
Call the cows home!
Louring storm clouds
Hitherward come;
East to West
Their wings are spread;
Lost in the blue
Is each heaven-high head;
They've dimmed the sun;
Turned day to night;
With a whistling wind
The woods are white;
Down streams the rain
On farm, barn, byre,
Bright green hill,
And bramble and briar,

Filling the valley
With glimmer and gloom:
Call the cows home!
Call the cows home!

To Mrs Reynolds's Cat

JOHN KEATS

Cat! who hast pass'd thy grand climacteric,
  How many mice and rats hast in thy days
  Destroy'd?—How many tit bits stolen? Gaze
With those bright languid segments green, and prick
Those velvet ears—but pr'ythee do not stick
  Thy latent talons in me—and upraise
  Thy gentle mew—and tell me all thy frays
Of fish and mice, and rats and tender chick.
Nay, look not down, nor lick thy dainty wrists—
  For all the wheezy asthma,—and for all
Thy tail's tip is nick'd off—and though the fists
  Of many a maid have given thee many a maul,
Still is that fur as soft as when the lists
  In youth thou enter'dst on glass bottled wall.

Up in the Morning Early

ROBERT BURNS

Cauld blaws the wind frae east to west,
  The drift is driving sairly;
Sae loud and shrill's I hear the blast—
  I'm sure it's winter fairly.

Up in the morning's no for me,
    Up in the morning early;
When a' the hills are covered wi' snaw,
    I'm sure it's winter fairly.

The birds sit chittering in the thorn,
    A' day they fare but sparely;
And lang's the night frae e'en to morn—
    I'm sure it's winter fairly.

Up in the morning's no for me,
    Up in the morning early;
When a' the hills are covered wi' snaw,
    I'm sure it's winter fairly.

Winter Warfare

EDGELL RICKWORD

Colonel Cold strode up the Line
    (tabs of rime and spurs of ice);
stiffened all who met his glare:
    horses, men, and lice.

Visited a forward post,
    left them burning, ear to foot;
fingers stuck to biting steel,
    toes to frozen boot.

Stalked on into No Man's Land,
    turned the wire to fleecy wool,
iron stakes to sugar sticks
    snapping at a pull.

Those who watched with hoary eyes
  saw two figures gleaming there;
Hauptmann Kalte, Colonel Cold,
  gaunt in the grey air.

Stiffly, tinkling spurs they moved,
  glassy eyed, with glinting heel
stabbing those who lingered there
  torn by screaming steel.

Christmas Eve: A Ceremonie

ROBERT HERRICK

Come guard this night the Christmas-pie,
That the Thiefe, though ne'r so slie,
With his flesh-hooks, don't come nigh
  To catch it.

From him who all alone sits there,
Having his eyes still in his eare,
And a deal of nightly fear
  To watch it.

Dance to your Daddy

ANONYMOUS

Dance to your daddy,
My little laddy.
Dance to your daddy,
My little man.
Thou shalt have a fish,
Thou shalt have a fin,
Thou shalt have a haddock
When the boat comes in.

Thou shalt have a codling,
Boilèd in a pan,
Dance to your daddy
My little man.
When thou art a man,
And fit to take a wife,
Thou shalt wed a maid
And love her all your life.
She shall be your lassie—
Thou shalt be her man.
Dance to your daddy
My little man.

Dearly Beloved Brethren

JOSEPH TABRAR

Dearly beloved brethren isn't it a sin
When you peel potatoes you throw away the skin,
The skins feed pigs and the pigs feed you:
Dearly beloved brethren is not that true?

Down by the Salley Gardens

W. B. YEATS

Down by the salley gardens my love and I did meet;
She passed the salley gardens with little snow-white feet.
She bid me take love easy, as the leaves grow on the tree;
But I, being young and foolish, with her would not agree.

In a field by the river my love and I did stand,
And on my leaning shoulder she laid her snow-white hand.
She bid me take life easy, as the grass grows on the weirs;
But I was young and foolish, and now am full of tears.

Tarra Ding Ding Ding Dido

ANONYMOUS

Down to the knees in blood, up to the knees in water,
  My boots are lined with gold, my stockings lined with silver;

A red rose on my breast, a gold ring on my finger,
  Tarra ding ding ding, tarra ding ding ding dido.

Down to the knees in blood, up to the knees in water,
  My boots are lined with gold, my stockings lined with silver;

I for the pots and pans, I for the man that made them,
  Tarra ding ding ding, tarra ding ding ding dido.

Shepherds' Counting Rhyme

ANONYMOUS

Eeny, teeny, ether, fether, fip,
  Satha, latha, ko, darthur, dick,
Ten-dick, teen-dick, ether-dick, fether-dick, bunkin,
  Een-bunkin, teen-bunkin, ether-bunkin, fether-bunkin, digit.

Winter Rain

CHRISTINA ROSSETTI

Every valley drinks,
    Every dell and hollow,
Where the kind rain sinks and sinks,
    Green of Spring will follow.

Yet a lapse of weeks—
    Buds will burst their edges,
Strip their wool-coats, glue-coats, streaks,
    In the woods and hedges;

Weave a bower of love
  For birds to meet each other,
Weave a canopy above
  Nest and egg and mother.

But for fattening rain
  We should have no flowers,
Never a bud or leaf again
  But for soaking showers....

Game Rhyme

ANONYMOUS

Green peas, mutton pies, tell me where my Maggie lies,
  I'll be there before she dies, green peas, mutton pies:
Three pairs of blankets, and four pairs of sheets,
  One yard of cotton to mend my Johnny's breeks.

Green peas, mutton pies, tell me where my Johnny lies,
  I'll be there before he dies and cuddle in his bosom.
Baby in the cradle, playing with the keys,
  Maggie in the pea park, picking up the peas.

The Eagle

ALFRED LORD TENNYSON

He clasps the crag with hookèd hands
Close to the sun in lonely lands;
Ring'd with the azure world he stands.
The wrinkled sea beneath him crawls;
He watches from his mountain walls,
And like a thunderbolt he falls.

Song from 'Charles the First'

P. B. SHELLEY

Heigho! the lark and the owl!
    One flies the morning, and one lulls the night:—
Only the nightingale, poor fond soul,
    Sings like the fool through darkness and light.

'A widow bird sate mourning for her love
    Upon a wintry bough;
The frozen wind crept on above,
    The freezing stream below.

'There was no leaf upon the forest bare,
    No flower upon the ground,
And little motion in the air
    Except the mill-wheel's sound.'

The House of Hospitalities

THOMAS HARDY

Here we broached the Christmas barrel,
    Pushed up the charred log-ends;
Here we sang the Christmas carol,
    And called in friends.

Time has tired me since we met here
    When the folk now dead were young
Since the viands were outset here
    And quaint songs sung.

And the worm has bored the viol
    That used to lead the tune,
Rust eaten out the dial
    That struck night's noon.

13

Now no Christmas brings in neighbours,
　And the New Year comes unlit;
Where we sang the mole now labours,
　And spiders knit.

Yet at midnight if here walking,
　When the moon sheets wall and tree,
I see forms of old time talking,
　Who smile on me.

Mary Ann

JOSEPH TABRAR

He's bought a bed and a table too,
A big tin dish for making stew,
A large flat-iron to iron his shirt,
And a flannel, and a scrubbing brush to wash away the dirt.
And he's bought a pail and basins three,
A coffee pot, a kettle, and a teapot for the tea,
　And a soap-bowl and a ladle,
　And a gridiron and a cradle,
And he's going to marry Mary Ann, that's me!
He's going to marry Mary Ann!

Counting out Rhyme

ANONYMOUS

Horcum borcum curious corkum
Herricum, berricam, buzz:
Eggs, butter, cheese, bread
Stick, stock, stone dead.

The Queen of Hearts

CHRISTINA ROSSETTI

How comes it, Flora, that, whenever we
Play cards together, you invariably,
   However the pack parts,
   Still hold the Queen of Hearts?

I've scanned you with a scrutinising gaze,
Resolved to fathom these your secret ways:
   But, sift them as I will,
   Your ways are secret still.

I cut and shuffle; shuffle, cut, again;
But all my cutting, shuffling, proves in vain:
   Vain hope, vain forethought too;
   That Queen still falls to you.

I dropped her once, prepense; but, ere the deal
Was dealt, your instinct seemed her loss to feel:
   'There should be one card more,'
   You said, and searched the floor.

I cheated once; I made a private notch
In Heart-Queen's back, and kept a lynx-eyed watch;
   Yet such another back
   Deceived me in the pack:

The Queen of Clubs assumed by arts unknown
An imitative dint that seemed my own;
   This notch, not of my doing,
   Misled me to my ruin.

It baffles me to puzzle out the clue,
Which must be skill, or craft, or luck in you:
   Unless, indeed, it be
   Natural affinity.

Ana-{MARY / ARMY} gram

GEORGE HERBERT

How well her name an *Army* doth present,
In whom the *Lord of hosts* did pitch his tent!

If all the World were Paper

ANONYMOUS

If all the world were paper
    If all the sea were ink,
If all the trees were bread and cheese,
    What would we have to drink?

If all the vessels ran,
    If none but had a crack,
If Spanish apes ate all the grapes,
    What would we do for sack?

If it's ever spring again

THOMAS HARDY

If it's ever spring again,
    Spring again,
I shall go where went I when
Down the moor-cock splashed, and hen,
Seeing me not, amid their flounder,
Standing with my arm around her;
If it's ever spring again,
    Spring again.
I shall go where went I then.

16

If it's ever summer-time,
    Summer-time,
With the hay crop at the prime,
And the cuckoos—two—in rhyme,
As they used to be, or seemed to,
We shall do as long we've dreamed to,
If it's ever summer-time,
    Summer-time,
With the hay, and bees achime.

If the Man who Turnip Cries

SAMUEL JOHNSON

If the man who turnip cries
Cry not when his father dies
'Tis a proof that he had rather
Have a turnip than a father.

The Song of the Old Mother

W. B. YEATS

I rise in the dawn, and I kneel and blow
Till the seed of the fire flicker and glow;
And then I must scrub and bake and sweep
Till stars are beginning to blink and peep;
And the young lie long and dream in their bed
Of the matching of ribbons for bosom and head,
And their day goes over in idleness,
And they sigh if the wind but lift a tress:
While I must work because I am old,
And the seed of the fire gets feeble and cold.

17

Cushie Butterfield

GEORGE RIDLEY

I's a broken-hearted keelman, and I's over head in love
With a young lass in Gateshead and I call her my dove.
Her name's Cushie Butterfield, and she sells yellow clay,
And her cousin is a muckman, and they call him Tom Grey.

> She's a big lass, and a bonny lass,
> And she likes her beer,
> And they call her Cushie Butterfield
> And I wish she was here.

Her eyes is like two holes in a blanket burnt through,
Her brows in a morning would spyen a young cow,
And when I hear her shouting, 'Will ye buy any clay?'
Like a candyman's trumpet, it steals my heart away.

Ye'll oft see her down at Sandgate when the fresh herring come in.
She's like a bag full of sawdust, tied round with a string.
She wears big galoshes too, and her stockings once was white,
And her petticoat's lilac, and her hat's never straight.

When I asked her to marry me she started to laugh;
'No! None of your monkey tricks, for I don't like such chaff.'
Then she starts a-blubbering, and she roared like a bull,
And the chaps on the Quay says I'm nowt but a fool.

She says the chap that gets her must work every day,
And when he comes home at nights he must go and seek clay;
And when he's away seeking, she'll make balls and sing
'Oh well may the keel row that my laddie's in.'

Miss T.

WALTER DE LA MARE

It's a very odd thing—
　As odd as can be—
That whatever Miss T. eats
　Turns into Miss T.;
Porridge and apples,
　Mince, muffins and mutton,
Jam, junket, jumbles—
　Not a rap, not a button
It matters; the moment
　They're out of her plate,
Though shared by Miss Butcher
　And sour Mr. Bate;
Tiny and cheerful,
　And neat as can be,
Whatever Miss T. eats
　Turns into Miss T.

A Little Boy Threw

ANONYMOUS

It snowed a mist, it snowed a mist,
It snowed all over the land:
Till all the boys throughout the town
Went out with ball in hand.

A little boy threw his ball so high,
He threw his ball so low;
He threw it into a dusky garden
Among the blades of snow.

19

'Come here, come here, you sweet little boy,
Come here and get your ball.'
'I'll not come here and I'll not come there,
And I'll not come in your hall.'

She showed him an apple as yellow as gold,
She showed him a bright gold ring,
She showed him a cherry as red as blood,
And that enticed him in;

Enticed him into the sitting room,
Enticed him into the kitchen,
And there he saw his own dear nurse
A-picking of a chicken.

'I'm washing this basin the livelong day,
To catch your heart's blood in;
And I won't spare you nor yet your ma,
Nor any of your kin.'

And she dragged him to the cooling board,
And stabbed him like a sheep,
And threw him into the dusky well,
With his grammar at his feet.

The Sandgate Girl's Lamentation

ANONYMOUS

I was a young maid truly,
And lived in Sandgate Street.
I thought to marry a good man
To keep me warm at neet.

He's an ugly body, a bubbly body,
An ill-fared, hideous loon;
And I have married a keelman,
And my good days are done.

I thought to marry a parson
To hear me say my prayers;
But I have married a keelman
And he kicks me down the stairs.

I thought to marry a dyer
To dye my apron blue;
But I have married a keelman
And he makes me sorely rue.

I thought to marry a joiner
To make me chair and stool;
But I have married a keelman
And he's a perfect fool.

I thought to marry a sailor
To bring me sugar and tea;
But I have married a keelman
And that he lets me see.

Poor Old Horse

ANONYMOUS

My clothing was once of the linsey woolsey fine,
My tail it grew at length, my coat did likewise shine;
But now I'm growing old; my beauty does decay,
My master frowns upon me; one day I heard him say,
                    Poor old horse: let him die.

Once I was kept in the stable snug and warm,
To keep my tender limbs from any cold or harm;
But now, in open fields, I am forced to go,
In all sorts of weather, let it be hail, rain, freeze, or snow.
Poor old horse: let him die.

Once I was fed on the very best corn and hay
That ever grew in yon fields, or in yon meadows gay;
But now there's no such doing can I find at all,
I'm glad to pick the green sprouts that grow behind yon wall.
Poor old horse: let him die.

'You are old, you are cold, you are deaf, dull, dumb and slow,
You are not fit for anything, or in my team to draw.
You have eaten all my hay, you have spoiled all my straw,
So hang him, whip, stick him, to the huntsman let him go.'
Poor old horse: let him die.

My hide unto the tanners then I would freely give,
My body to the hound dogs, I would rather die than live,
Likewise my poor old bones that have carried you many a mile,
Over hedges, ditches, brooks, bridges, likewise gates and stiles.
Poor old horse: let him die.

The Little Black Boy

WILLIAM BLAKE

My mother bore me in the southern wild,
And I am black, but O! my soul is white;
White as an angel is the English child,
But I am black, as if bereav'd of light.

My mother taught me underneath a tree,
And sitting down before the heat of day,
She took me on her lap and kissed me,
And pointing to the east, began to say:

'Look on the rising sun: there God does live,
And gives his light, and gives his heat away;
And flowers and trees and beasts and men receive
Comfort in morning, joy in the noonday.

'And we are put on earth a little space,
That we may learn to bear the beams of love;
And these black bodies and this sunburnt face
Is but a cloud, and like a shady grove.

'For when our souls have learn'd the heat to bear,
The cloud will vanish; we shall hear his voice,
Saying: "Come out from the grove, my love & care,
And round my golden tent like lambs rejoice."'

Thus did my mother say, and kissed me;
And thus I say to little English boy:
When I from black and he from white cloud free,
And round the tent of God like lambs we joy,

I'll shade him from the heat, till he can bear
To lean in joy upon our father's knee;
And then I'll stand and stroke his silver hair,
And be like him, and he will then love me.

The Flying Cloud

ANONYMOUS

My name is Edward Holland
As you may understand
I belong to the country of Waterford
Near Eirings happy land

When I was young and in my prime
And fortune on me smiled
My parents reared me tenderly
I being their only child

My father bound me to a trade
In Waterford's own town
He bound me to a cooper there
By the name of William Brown

I served my master faithfully
For eighteen months or more
Till I shipped aboard the Ocean Queen
Bound down for Bermuda's shore

When we arrived at Bermuda shore
I fell in with a Capting More,
The commander of the Flying Cloud
And belonging to Trymore.

He questioned and cross questioned me
On a slaving voyage to go
To the burning shores of Africa
Where the sugar cane does grow.

Now three or four weeks after this
We arrived at the African shore
And eighteen hundred of those poor souls
From their native land we bore.

We would march them on our quarterdecks
And store them down below.
It was eighteen inches to a man;
It was what they had to go.

We sailed away without delay
With our cargo of slaves.
It would have been better for them poor souls
Had they been in their graves.

The plaguey fever came aboard
Swept half of them away
We dragged their dead bodies on deck
And threw them in the sea.

Now two or three weeks after this
We arrived at Bermuda shore
Where we sold them to the planters there
To be slaves for evermore.

The rye and coffee fields to hoe
Beneath the burning sun
For to live a long and dreary life
'Till their career was run.

Now when our slaving money was all gone
We put to sea again.
When Capting More he came on deck
And said to us his men,

'There is gold and silver to be had
If you will agree with me,
We will hoist aloft the pirate flag
And scour the raging sea.'

Now they all agreed excepting five
And those we had to land.
Two of them being Boston boys,
Two more from Newfoundland.

The other being an Irish man
Belonging to Trymore.
I wish to God I had joined those five
And went with them on shore.

Now we robbed and plundered many the ship
Down on the Spanish Main
Caused many the widow and orphan child
In sorrow to remain.

We would march them on the quarterdecks
Give them a watery grave
For the saying of that Capting More
That a dead man tells no tales.

Now chased were we by many a ship
Both frigates and liners too.
It was all in vain astern of us
Their bomb shells they did throw.

It was all in vain astern of us
Their cannons roared aloud.
It was all in vain for to ever try
For to catch the Flying Cloud.

Now the Flying Cloud was a Spanish ship
Five thousand tons or more.
She would easily outsail any ship
Coming out of Baltimore.

Her sails were as white as the driven snow
On them there were no stains.
With a forty-nine brass pounder gun
She would carry an after main.

Now the Flying Cloud was as fine a ship
As ever swam the sea.
Or ever spread a main top sail
Before a pleasant breeze.

Now often have I watched that ship
As she went sailing by
With her royal galyants spread aloft
Above the canvas high.

Now a Spanish ship, the man of war
Her dungeon hove in view.
She fired a shot acrost our deck
As a signal to heave to.

But to her we paid no attention
As before a pleasant breeze
Till a chance shot cut our mainmast down
We then soon fell behind.

We cleared our decks for action
As she ranged up alongside.
And soon acrost our quarterdecks
There flowed a crimson tide.

We fought till Capting More was slain
And eight of our men
Till a bombshell set our ship on fire
We were forced to surrender then.

It's now to Newgate we are brought
Bound down in iron bands
For the murdering and plundering of many the ship
Down on the ocean strand.

It's drinking and bad company
That's made a wretch of me.
Come all young men a warning take
Bid a curse to the pirate sea.

Lament of Hsi-Chun

Translated by Arthur Waley

About the year 105 B.C. a Chinese lady named Hsi-Chun was sent to be the wife of a central Asian nomad king, K'un Mo, king of the Wu-sun. When she got there, she found her husband was old and decrepit. He only saw her once or twice a year when they drank a cup of wine together. They could not talk as they had no language in common.

My people have married me
In a far corner of Earth;
Sent me away to a strange land,
To the king of the Wu-sun.
A tent is my house,
Of felt are my walls;
Raw flesh my food
With mare's milk to drink.
Always thinking of my own country,
My heart sad within.
Would I were a yellow stork
And could fly to my old home!

Fine Work with Pitch and Copper

WILLIAM CARLOS WILLIAMS

Now they are resting
in the fleckless light
separately in unison

like the sacks
of sifted stone stacked
regularly by twos

about the flat roof
ready after lunch
to be opened and strewn

The copper in eight
foot strips has been
beaten lengthwise

down the center at right
angles and lies ready
to edge the coping

One still chewing
picks up a copper strip
and runs eye along it

Oats and Beans and Barley

ANONYMOUS

Oats and beans and barley grow!
Oats and beans and barley grow!
Do you or I or anyone know
How oats and beans and barley grow?

First the farmer sows his seed,
Then he stands and takes his ease,
Stamps his foot and *claps* his hands,
And *turns around* to view the land.
Waiting for a partner,
Waiting for a partner!
Open the ring and take one in!

Now you are married you must obey,
You must be true to all you say.
You must be kind, you must be good
And help your wife to chop the wood!

Lovewell's Fight

ANONYMOUS

Of worthy Captain Lovewell, I purpose now to sing,
How valiantly he served his country and his King;
He and his valiant soldiers, did range the woods full wide,
And hardships they endured to quell the Indians' pride.

'Twas nigh unto Pigwacket, on the eighth day of May,
They spied a rebel Indian soon after break of day;
He on a bank was walking, upon a neck of land,
Which leads into a pond as we're made to understand.

Our men resolv'd to have him and travell'd two miles round,
Until they met the Indian, who boldly stood his ground;
Then spake up Captain Lovewell, 'Take you good heed,' says he,
'This rogue is to decoy us, I very plainly see.'

'The Indians lie in ambush, in some place nigh at hand,
In order to surround us upon this neck of land;
Therefore we'll march in order, and each man leave his pack,
That we may briskly fight them when they make their attack.'

They came unto this Indian, who did them this defy,
As soon as they came nigh him, two guns did he let fly,
Which wounded Captain Lovewell, and likewise one man more,
But when this rogue was running, they laid him in his gore.

Then having scalp'd the Indian, they went back to the spot,
Where they had laid their packs down, but there they
found them not,
For the Indians having spy'd them, when they them
down did lay,
Did seize them for their plunder, and carry them away.

These rebels lay in ambush, this very place hard by,
So that an English soldier did one of them espy,
And cried out 'Here's an Indian,' with that they started out,
As fiercely as old lions, and hideously did shout.

With that our valiant English, all gave a loud huzza,
To shew the rebel Indians they fear'd them not a straw;
So now the fight began, and as fiercely as could be,
The Indians ran up to them, but soon were forc'd to flee.

Then spake up Captain Lovewell, when first the fight began,
'Fight on my valiant heroes! You see they fall like rain.'
For as we are inform'd, the Indians were so thick,
A man could scarcely fire a gun and not some of them hit.

Then did the rebels try their best our soldiers to surround,
But they could not accomplish it, because there was a pond,
To which our men retreated and covered all the rear,
The rogues were forc'd to flee them, altho' they skulk'd for fear.

Two logs there were behind them, that close together lay,
Without being discovered, they could not get away,
Therefore our valiant English, they travell'd in a row,
And at a handsome distance as they were wont to go.

31

'Twas 10 o'clock in the morning, when first the fight begun,
And fiercely did continue until the setting sun,
Excepting that the Indians, some hours before 'twas night,
Drew off into the bushes and ceased awhile to fight.

But soon again returned, in fierce and furious mood,
Shouting as in the morning, but not yet half so loud;
For as we are informed, so thick and fast they fell,
Scarce twenty of their number at night did get home well.

And that our valiant English, till midnight there did stay,
To see whether the rebels would have another fray;
But they no more returning, they made off towards their home,
And brought away their wounded as far as they could come.

Of all our valiant English, there were but thirty-four,
And of the rebel Indians, there were about four score.
And sixteen of our English did safely home return,
The rest were killed and wounded, for which we all must mourn.

Our worthy Captain Lovewell among them there did die,
They killed Lt. Robins, and wounded good young Frye,
Who was our English chaplain; he many Indians slew,
And some of them he scalp'd when bullets round him flew.

Young Fullam too I'll mention, because he fought so well,
Endeavouring to save a man, a sacrifice he fell;
But yet our valiant Englishmen in fight were ne'er dismay'd,
But still they kept their motion, and Wyman's Captain made.

Who shot the old chief Paugus, which did the foe defeat,
Then set his men in order, and brought off the retreat;
And braving many dangers and hardships in the way,
They safe arriv'd at Dunstable, the thirteenth day of May.

Goody Blake and Harry Gill

WILLIAM WORDSWORTH

Oh! what's the matter? what's the matter?
What is't that ails young Harry Gill?
That evermore his teeth they chatter,
Chatter, chatter, chatter still!
Of waistcoats Harry has no lack,
Good duffle grey, and flannel fine;
He has a blanket on his back,
And coats enough to smother nine.

In March, December, and in July,
'Tis all the same with Harry Gill;
The neighbours tell, and tell you truly,
His teeth they chatter, chatter still.
At night, at morning, and at noon,
'Tis all the same with Harry Gill;
Beneath the sun, beneath the moon,
His teeth they chatter, chatter still!

Young Harry was a lusty drover,
And who so stout of limb as he?
His cheeks were red as ruddy clover:
His voice was like the voice of three.
Old Goody Blake was old and poor;
Ill fed she was, and thinly clad;
And any man who passed her door
Might see how poor a hut she had.

All day she spun in her poor dwelling:
And then her three hours' work at night,
Alas! 'twas hardly worth the telling,
It would not pay for candle-light.

33

Remote from sheltered village green,
On a hill's northern side she dwelt,
Where from sea-blasts the hawthorns lean
And hoary dews are slow to melt.

By the same fire to boil their pottage,
Two poor old Dames, as I have known,
Will often live in one small cottage;
But she, poor Woman! housed alone.
'Twas well enough when summer came,
The long, warm, lightsome summer-day,
Then at her door the *canty* Dame
Would sit, as any linnet gay.

But when the ice our streams did fetter,
Oh then how her old bones would shake!
You would have said, if you had met her,
'Twas a hard time for Goody Blake.
Her evenings then were dull and dead:
Sad case it was, as you may think,
For very cold to go to bed;
And then for cold not sleep a wink.

O joy for her! whene'er in winter
The winds at night had made a rout;
And scattered many a lusty splinter
And many a rotten bough about.
Yet never had she, well or sick,
As every man who knew her says,
A pile beforehand, turf or stick,
Enough to warm her for three days.

Now, when the frost was past enduring,
And made her poor old bones to ache,
Could any thing be more alluring
Than an old hedge to Goody Blake?

34

And, now and then, it must be said,
When her old bones were cold and chill,
She left her fire, or left her bed,
To seek the hedge of Harry Gill.

Now Harry he had long suspected
This trespass of old Goody Blake;
And vowed that she should be detected—
That he on her would vengeance take.
And oft from his warm fire he'd go,
And to the fields his road would take;
And there, at night, in frost and snow,
He watched to seize old Goody Blake.

And once, behind a rick of barley,
Thus looking out did Harry stand:
The moon was full and shining clearly,
And crisp with frost the stubble land.
—He hears a noise—he's all awake—
Again?—on tip-toe down the hill
He softly creeps—'tis Goody Blake.
She's at the hedge of Harry Gill!

Right glad was he when he beheld her:
Stick after stick did Goody pull:
He stood behind a bush of elder,
Till she had filled her apron full.
When with her load she turned about,
The by-way back again to take;
He started forward, with a shout,
And sprang upon poor Goody Blake.

And fiercely by the arm he took her,
And by the arm he held her fast,
And fiercely by the arm he shook her,
And cried, 'I've caught you then at last!'

Then Goody, who had nothing said,
Her bundle from her lap let fall;
And, kneeling on the sticks she prayed,
To God that is the judge of all.

She prayed, her withered hand uprearing,
While Harry held her by the arm—
'God! who art never out of hearing,
O may he never more be warm!'
The cold, cold moon above her head,
Thus on her knees did Goody pray;
Young Harry heard what she had said:
And icy cold he turned away.

He went complaining all the morrow
That he was cold and very chill:
His face was gloom, his heart was sorrow,
Alas! that day for Harry Gill!
That day he wore a riding-coat,
But not a whit the warmer he:
Another was on Thursday brought,
And ere the Sabbath he had three.

'Twas all in vain, a useless matter,
And blankets were about him pinned;
Yet still his jaws and teeth they clatter
Like a loose casement in the wind.
And Harry's flesh it fell away;
And all who see him say, 'tis plain,
That, live as long as live he may,
He never will be warm again.

No word to any man he utters,
A-bed or up, to young or old;
But ever to himself he mutters,
'Poor Harry Gill is very cold.'

A-bed or up, by night or day;
His teeth they chatter, chatter, still.
Now think, ye farmers all, I pray,
Of Goody Blake and Harry Gill!

Tillie

WALTER DE LA MARE

Old Tillie Turveycombe
Sat to sew,
Just where a patch of fern did grow;
There, as she yawned,
And yawn wide did she,
Floated some seed
Down her gull-e-t;
And look you once,
And look you twice,
Poor old Tillie
Was gone in a trice.
But oh, when the wind
Do a-moaning come,
'Tis poor old Tillie
Sick for home;
And oh, when a voice
In the mist do sigh,
Old Tillie Turveycombe's
Floating by.

The Big Rock Candy Mountains

ANONYMOUS

One evenin' as the sun went down
And the jungle fire was burnin',
Down the track came a hobo hikin',
And he said: 'Boys, I'm not turnin',
I'm headed fer a land that's far away
Beside the crystal fountains,
So come with me, we'll all go see
The Big Rock Candy Mountains.'

In the Big Rock Candy Mountains,
There's a land that's fair and bright,
Where the handouts grow on bushes,
And you sleep out every night.
Where the boxcars are all empty,
And the sun shines every day
On the birds and the bees and the cigarette trees,
And the lemonade springs where the bluebird sings,
In the Big Rock Candy Mountains.

In the Big Rock Candy Mountains,
All the cops have wooden legs,
The bulldogs all have rubber teeth,
And the hens lay soft-boiled eggs.
The farmers' trees are full of fruit,
And the barns are full of hay.
Oh, I'm bound to go where there ain't no snow,
Where the rain don't pour, the wind don't blow,
In the Big Rock Candy Mountains.

In the Big Rock Candy Mountains,
You never change your socks,
And the little streams of alcohol
Come tricklin' down the rocks.

There the brakemen have to tip their hats
And the railroad bulls are blind.
There's a lake of stew and of whisky too,
You can paddle all around 'em in a big canoe,
In the Big Rock Candy Mountains.

In the Big Rock Candy Mountains,
All the jails are made of tin,
And you can bust right out again
As soon as you are in.
There ain't no short-handled shovels,
No axes, saws or picks.
I'm goin' to stay where you sleep all day,
Where they hung the Turk that invented work,
In the Big Rock Candy Mountains.

One Two Three

ANONYMOUS

One two three
    Father caught a flea:
Put it in the teapot
    To make a cup of tea.

Thaw

EDWARD THOMAS

Over the land freckled with snow half-thawed
The speculating rooks at their nests cawed
And saw from elm-tops, delicate as flower of grass,
What we below could not see, Winter pass.

Frying Pan's Theology

A. B. PATERSON

SCENE: On Monaro.
  Dramatis Personae:
Shock-headed blackfellow,
  Boy (on a pony).

Snowflakes are falling
  Gentle and slow,
Youngster says, 'Frying Pan
  What makes it snow?'

Frying Pan, confident,
  Makes the reply—
'Shake 'im big flour bag
  Up in the sky!'

'What! when there's miles of it?
  Surely that's brag.
Who is there strong enough
  Shake such a bag?'

'What parson tellin' you,
  Ole Mister Dodd,
Tell you in Sunday-school?
  Big pfeller God!

'Him drive 'im bullock dray,
  Then thunder go;
Him shake 'im flour bag—
  Tumble down snow!'

Lady Maisry

ANONYMOUS

She called to her little page-boy,
Who was her brother's son;
She told him as quick as he could go,
To bring her lord safe home.

Now the very first mile he would walk,
And the second he would run,
And when he came to a broken broken bridge
He bent his breast and swum.

Now when he came to the New Castel
The lord was set at meat
'If you were to know as much as I
How little would you eat.'

'O is my tower falling down?
Or does my bower burn?
Or is my lady lighter yet
Of a daughter or a son?'

'O no your tower is not falling down,
Nor does your bower burn:
But we are afraid ere you return
Your lady will be dead and gone.'

'Come servant saddle my milk-white steed!
Come saddle my pony too!
That I may neither eat nor drink
Till I come to the Old Castel!'

Now when he came to the Old Castel
He heard a big bell toll,
And then he saw his noble noblemen
A-bearing of a pall.

'Lay down, lay down that gentle gentle corpse'
(As it lay fast asleep)
'That I may kiss her red ruby lips
Which I used to kiss so sweet!'

Six times he kissed her red ruby lips,
Nine times he kissed her chin,
Ten times he kissed her snowy snowy breast,
Where love did enter in.

The lady was buried on that Sunday
Before the prayer begun:
And the lord he died on the next Sunday
Before the prayer was done.

Hailstorm in May

GERARD MANLEY HOPKINS

Strike, churl; hurl, cheerless wind, then; heltering hail
May's beauty massacre and wispèd wild clouds grow
Out on the giant air; tell Summer No,
Bid joy back, have at the harvest, keep Hope pale.

Vertue

GEORGE HERBERT

Sweet day, so cool, so calm, so bright,
The bridall of the earth and skie:
The dew shall weep thy fall to night;
        For thou must die.

Sweet rose, whose hue angrie and brave
Bids the rash gazer wipe his eye:
Thy root is ever in its grave,
               And thou must die.

Sweet spring, full of sweet dayes and roses,
A box where sweets compacted lie;
My musick shows ye have your closes,
               And all must die.

Onely a sweet and vertuous soul,
Like season'd timber, never gives;
But though the whole world turn to coal,
               Then chiefly lives.

Tall Nettles

EDWARD THOMAS

Tall nettles cover up, as they have done
These many springs, the rusty harrow, the plough
Long worn out, and the roller made of stone:
Only the elm butt tops the nettles now.

This corner of the farmyard I like most:
As well as any bloom upon a flower
I like the dust on the nettles, never lost
Except to prove the sweetness of a shower.

The Crows Kept Flyin'

ANONYMOUS

The crows kept flyin' up, boys,
The crows kept flyin' up.
The dog he seen and whimpered, boys,
Though he was but a pup.

The lost was found, we brought him round
And took him from the place,
While the ants was swarming on the ground,
And the crows was sayin' grace.

The 23 Psalme

GEORGE HERBERT

The God of love my shepherd is,
    And he that doth me feed:
While he is mine, and I am his,
    What can I want or need?

He leads me to the tender grasse,
    Where I both feed and rest;
Then to the streams that gently passe:
    In both I have the best.

Or if I stray, he doth convert
    And bring my minde in frame:
And all this not for my desert,
    But for his holy name.

Yea, in deaths shadie black abode
    Well may I walk, not fear:
For thou art with me; and thy rod
    To guide, thy staffe to bear.

Nay, thou dost make me sit and dine,
    Ev'n in my enemies sight:
My head with oyl, my cup with wine
    Runnes over day and night.

Surely thy sweet and wondrous love
 Shall measure all my dayes;
And as it never shall remove,
 So neither shall my praise.

The Heron

ANONYMOUS

The heron flew east, the heron flew west,
She bore her over the fair forest.
Lully, lullay; lully, lullay;
The falcon hath stolen my mate away.

She bore her up, she bore her down,
She bore her over the heath so brown.

She bore her over the meadows green,
And all to espy what might be seen.

O, then she saw an orchard fair,
Where groweth many an apple and pear.

And in that orchard there standeth a hall,
That hangèd was with purple and pall.

And in that hall there standeth a bower,
Was all clad over with lily flower.

And in that bower there standeth a bed,
With silken sheets and gold so red.

And in that bed there lieth a knight,
Whose wounds are bleeding both day and night.

And under that bed there runneth a flood,
Was half of water and half of blood.

45

And by that bed there standeth a stone,
And a leal maiden was set thereon.

With silver needle and silken thread,
Stemming the wounds where they did bleed.
Lully, lullay; lully, lullay;
The falcon hath stolen my mate away.

Autumn Change

JOHN CLARE

The leaves of autumn drop by twos and threes,
And the black cloud hung o'er the old low church
Is fixed as is a rock that never stirs.
But look again and you may well perceive
The weathercock is in another sky,
And the cloud passing leaves the blue behind.

Crimson and yellow, blotched with iron-brown,
The autumn tans and variegates the leaves;
The nuts are ripe in woods about the town;
Russet the cleared fields where the bindweed weaves
Round stubbles and still flowers; the trefoil seeds
And troubles all the lands. From rig to furrow
There's nothing left but rubbish and foul weeds.
I love to see the rabbits' snug-made burrow
Under the old hedge-bank or huge mossed oak
Claspt fast with ivy—there the rabbit breeds
Where the kite peelews and the ravens croak
And hares and rabbits at their leisure feed,
As varying autumn through her changes runs,
Season of sudden storms and brilliant suns.

The Little Cart

CH'ÊN TSŬ-LUNG

Translated by Arthur Waley

The little cart jolting and banging through the
                              yellow haze of dusk;
The man pushing behind, the woman pulling in front.
They have left the city and do not know where to go.
'Green, green, those elm-tree leaves; *they* will cure
                              my hunger,
If only we could find some quiet place and sup
                              on them together.'

The wind has flattened the yellow mother-wort;
Above it in the distance they see walls of a house.
'*There* surely must be people living who'll give you
                              something to eat.'
They tap at the door, but no one comes; they look in,
                              but the kitchen is empty.
They stand hesitating in the lonely road and their tears
                              fall like rain.

The Maidens Came

ANONYMOUS

The maidens came
When I was in my mother's bower;
I had all that I would.
   The bailey beareth the bell away;
   The lily, the rose, the rose I lay.

47

The silver is white, red is the gold;
The robes they lay in fold.
    The bailey beareth the bell away;
    The lily, the rose, the rose I lay.

And through the glass window shines the sun.
How should I love, and I so young?
    The bailey beareth the bell away;
    The lily, the rose, the rose I lay.

Charm

BEN JONSON

The owl is abroad, the bat, and the toad,
    And so is the cat-a-mountain;
The ant and the mole sit both in a hole,
    And the frog peeps out o' the fountain.
The dogs they do bay, and the timbrels play,
    The spindle is now a-turning;
The moon it is red, and the stars are fled,
    But all the sky is a-burning:
The ditch is made, and our nails the spade,
With pictures full, of wax and of wool;
Their livers I stick with needles quick;
There lacks but the blood to make up the flood.
Quickly, dame, then, bring your part in!
Spur, spur, upon little Martin,
Merrily, merrily, make him sail,
A worm in his mouth and a thorn in his tail,
Fire above, and fire below,
With a whip in your hand, to make him go!

A Tale

EDWARD THOMAS

There once the walls
Of the ruined cottage stood.
The periwinkle crawls
With flowers in its hair into the wood.

In flowerless hours
Never will the bank fail,
With everlasting flowers
On fragments of blue plates, to tell the tale.

There was a Man of Double Deed

ANONYMOUS

There was a man of double deed
Who sowed his garden full of seed;
And when the seed began to grow,
'Twas like a garden full of snow;
And when the snow began to fall,
Like birds it was upon the wall;
And when the birds began to fly,
'Twas like a shipwreck in the sky;
And when the sky began to crack,
'Twas like a stick upon my back;
And when my back began to smart,
'Twas like a pen-knife in my heart;
And when my heart began to bleed,
Then I was dead—and dead indeed.

The Sun has Long Been Set

WILLIAM WORDSWORTH

The sun has long been set,
  The stars are out by twos and threes,
The little birds are piping yet
  Among the bushes and trees;
There's a cuckoo, and one or two thrushes,
And a far-off wind that rushes,
And a sound of water that gushes,
And the cuckoo's sovereign cry
Fills all the hollow of the sky.
  Who would go parading
In London, and masquerading
On such a night of June
With that beautiful soft half-moon,
And all these innocent blisses?
On such a night as this is!

Last Week in October

THOMAS HARDY

The trees are undressing, and fling in many places—
On the gray road, the roof, the window-sill—
Their radiant robes and ribbons and yellow laces;
A leaf each second so is flung at will,
Here, there, another and another, still and still.

A spider's web has caught one while downcoming,
That stays there dangling when the rest pass on;
Like a suspended criminal hangs he, mumming
In golden garb, while one yet green, high yon,
Trembles, as fearing such a fate for himself anon.

They call me Hanging Johnny

ANONYMOUS

They call me Hanging Johnny—
Away, boys, away!
They say I hanged up many—
Then hang, boys, hang!

They say I hanged my brother—
Away, boys, away!
They say I hanged my mother—
Then hang, boys, hang!

They say I hanged my Annie—
Away, boys, away!
I hanged her up so canny—
Then hang, boys, hang!

They say I hanged my daddy—
Away, boys, away!
But I never hanged no body—
Then hang, boys, hang!

Upon a Spider Catching a Fly

EDWARD TAYLOR

Thou sorrow, venom Elfe:
  Is this thy play,
To spin a web out of thyselfe
  To Catch a Fly?
    For why?

51

I saw a pettish wasp
   Fall foule therein:
Whom yet thy whorle pins did not hasp
   Lest he should fling
      His sting.

But as afraid, remote
   Didst stand hereat,
And with thy little finger stroke
   And gently tap
      His back.

Thus gently him didst treate
   Lest he should pet,
And in a froppish, aspish heate
   Should greatly fret
      Thy net.

Whereas the silly Fly,
   Caught by its leg,
Thou by the throate took'st hastily,
   And 'hinde the head
      Bite Dead.

This goes to pot, that not
   Nature doth call.
Strive not above what strength hath got,
   Lest in the brawle
      Thou fall.

This Fray seems thus to us:
   Hells Spider gets
His intrails spun to whip Cords thus,
   And wove to nets,
      And sets.

To tangle Adams race
    In's stratagems
To their Destructions, Spoil'd, made base
    By venom things,
        Damn'd Sins.

Three Little Tailors

ANONYMOUS

Three little tailors dancing in a lantern
For a bit of candle;
Candle, lantern,
For a bit of candle;
Lantern, candle,
For a bit of candle.

The Book-Worms

ROBERT BURNS

Through and through th' inspired leaves,
    Ye maggots, make your windings;
But O respect his lordship's taste,
    And spare the golden bindings.

Digging

EDWARD THOMAS

To-day I think
Only with scents,—scents dead leaves yield,
And bracken, and wild carrot's seed,
And the square mustard field;

53

Odours that rise
When the spade wounds the root of tree,
Rose, currant, raspberry, or goutweed,
Rhubarb or celery;

The smoke's smell, too,
Flowing from where a bonfire burns
The dead, the waste, the dangerous,
And all to sweetness turns.

It is enough
To smell, to crumble the dark earth,
While the robin sings over again
Sad songs of Autumn mirth.

The Golden Vanity

ANONYMOUS

'Twas all on board a ship down in a southern sea,
And she goes by the name of the 'Golden Vanity';
I'm afraid that she'll be taken by this Spanish crew,
  As she sails along the Lowlands,
  As she sails along the Lowlands low.

Then up speaks our saucy cabin boy, without fear or joy,
Saying, 'What will you give me, if I will her destroy?'
'I'll give you gold and silver, my daughter fine and gay,
  If you'll destroy her in the Lowlands,
  If you'll sink her in the Lowlands low.'

The boy filled his chest and so boldly leaped in,
The boy filled his chest and then began to swim;
He swam alongside of the bold Spanish ship,
  And he sank her in the Lowlands,
  And he sank her in the Lowlands low.

Some were playing cards and some were playing dice,
And some were in their hammocks sleeping very nice;
He bored two holes into her side, he let the water in,
And he sank her in the Lowlands,
And he sank her in the Lowlands low.

The boy then swam back unto our good ship's side,
And being much exhausted, bitterly he cried,
'Captain, take me in, for I'm going with the tide,
And I'm sinking in the Lowlands,
And I'm sinking in the Lowlands low.'

'I will not take you in', our captain then replied,
'I'll shoot you and I'll stab you and I'll sink you in the tide,
And I'll sink you in the Lowlands,
And I'll sink you in the Lowlands low.'

The boy then swam around next the larboard side,
And being more exhausted, bitterly he cried,
'Messmates, take me in, for I'm going with the tide,
And I'm sinking in the Lowlands,
And I'm sinking in the Lowlands low.'

They hove the boy a rope and they hoisted him on deck,
They laid him on the quarter deck, the boy here soon died;
They sewed him up in canvas sack, they hove him in the tide,
And they buried him in the Lowlands,
And they buried him in the Lowlands low.

Urry, Urry, angry Ann

ANONYMOUS

Urry, urry, angry Ann,
Mulberry wax and tarry tan:
Ink stink stidlum stew
Nobody out but only you.

The Pettichap's Nest

JOHN CLARE

Well! in my many walks I've rarely found
A place less likely for a bird to form
Its nest—close by the rut-gulled wagon-road,
And on the almost bare foot-trodden ground,
With scarce a clump of grass to keep it warm!
Where not a thistle spreads its spears abroad,
Or prickly bush, to shield it from harm's way;
And yet so snugly made, that none may spy
It out, save peradventure. You and I
Had surely passed it in our walk today,
Had chance not led us by it!—Nay, e'en now,
Had not the old bird heard us trampling by
And fluttered out, we had not seen it lie,
Brown as the roadway side. Small bits of hay
Plucked from the old propt haystack's pleachy brow,
And withered leaves, make up its outward wall,
Which from the gnarled oak-dotterel yearly fall,
And in the old hedge-bottom rot away.
Built like an oven, through a little hole,
Scarcely admitting e'en two fingers in,
Hard to discern, the birds snug entrance win.
'Tis lined with feathers warm as silken stole,
Softer than seats of down for painless ease,
And full of eggs scarce bigger even than peas!
Here's one most delicate, with spots as small
As dust and of a faint and pinky red.
We'll let them be, and safety guard them well;
For fear's rude paths around are thickly spread,
And they are left to many dangerous ways.
A green grasshopper's jump might break the shells,
Yet lowing oxen pass them morn and night,

And restless sheep around them hourly stray;
And no grass springs but hungry horses bite,
That trample past them twenty times a day.
Yet, like a miracle, in safety's lap
They still abide unhurt, and out of sight.
Stop! here's the bird—that woodman at the gap
Frightened him from the hedge: 'tis olive-green.
Well! I declare it is the pettichap!
Not bigger than the wren, and seldom seen.
I've often found her nest in chance's way,
When I in pathless woods did idly roam;
But never did I dream until today
A spot like this would be her chosen home.

Song

WILLIAM SHAKESPEARE

When icicles hang by the wall
  And Dick the shepherd blows his nail,
And Tom bears logs into the hall,
  And milk comes frozen home in pail;
When blood is nipt, and ways be foul,
Then nightly sings the staring owl
      Tu-whoo!
To-whit, Tu-whoo! A merry note!
While greasy Joan doth keel the pot.

When all about the wind doth blow,
  And coughing drowns the parson's saw,
And birds sit brooding in the snow,
  And Marian's nose looks red and raw;

When roasted crabs hiss in the bowl—
Then nightly sings the staring owl
Tu-whoo!
To-whit, Tu-whoo! A merry note!
While greasy Joan doth keel the pot.

The Good Old Man

ANONYMOUS

Where are you going, my good old man?
Where are you going, my good old man?
Where are you going, my honey, my love, my dove?
The best old soul in the world.
Going to the town.

What are you going to buy, my good old man?
New dress.

How much will it cost, my good old man?
Fifty cents.

What do you want for supper, my good old man?
Sack of potatoes.

Potatoes will kill you, my good old man?
Don't care; want to die anyhow.

Where do you want to be buried, my good old man?
In the chimney-corner.

Ashes'll fall on you, my good old man?
Don't care if they do,
So I'm close to you.

Summer

CHRISTINA ROSSETTI

Winter is cold-hearted,
Spring is yea and nay,
Autumn is a weather-cock
  Blown every way:
Summer days for me
When every leaf is on its tree.

When Robin's not a beggar,
And Jenny Wren's a bride,
And larks hang singing, singing, singing,
  Over the wheat-fields wide,
  And anchored lilies ride,
  And the pendulum spider
Swings from side to side.

And blue-black beetles transact business,
  And gnats fly in a host,
And furry caterpillars hasten
  That no time be lost,
  And moths grow fat and thrive,
  And ladybirds arrive.
Before green apples blush,
Before green nuts embrown,
Why one day in the country
Is worth a month in town;
Is worth a day and a year
Of the dusty, musty, lag-fast fashion.

Cocky Robin

ANONYMOUS

Who killed Cocky Robin?
Who killed Cocky Robin?
Me, says the sparrow,
With my little bow and arrow,
It was I, it was I.

Who seen him die?
Me, says the fly,
With my little teenty eye.
It was I, it was I.

Who caught his blood?
Me, says the fish,
With my little silver dish.

Who made the coffin?
Me, says the crane,
With my little narrow plane.

Who made the shroud-en?
Me, says the eagle,
With my little fine needle.

Who dug his grave?
Me, says the crow,
With my little spade and hoe.

Who hauled him to it?
Me, says the lark,
With my little horse and cart.

Who let him down?
Me, says the flea,
With my little limber knee.

Who pat his grave?
Me, says the duck,
With my big splatter foot.

Who preached his funeral?
Me, says the swallow,
Just as loud as I could holloa.

Charms and Knots

GEORGE HERBERT

Who reade a chapter when they rise,
Shall ne're be troubled with ill eyes.

A poore man's rod, when thou dost ride,
Is both a weapon and a guide.

Who shuts his hand, hath lost his gold:
Who opens it, hath it twice told.

Who goes to bed and doth not pray,
Maketh two nights to ev'ry day.

Who by aspersions throw a stone
At th' head of others, hit their own.

Who looks on ground with humble eyes,
Findes himself there, and seeks to rise.

When th' hair is sweet through pride or lust,
The powder doth forget the dust...

In shallow waters heav'n doth show;
But who drinks on, to hell may go.

Stopping by Woods on a Snowy Evening

ROBERT FROST

Whose woods these are I think I know.
His house is in the village though;
He will not see me stopping here
To watch his woods fill up with snow.

My little horse must think it queer
To stop without a farmhouse near
Between the woods and frozen lake
The darkest evening of the year.

He gives his harness bells a shake
To ask if there is some mistake.
The only other sound's the sweep
Of easy wind and downy flake.

The woods are lovely, dark and deep.
But I have promises to keep,
And miles to go before I sleep,
And miles to go before I sleep.

'You are old, Father William'

C. L. DODGSON (LEWIS CARROLL)

'You are old, Father William,' the young man said,
  'And your hair has become very white;
And yet you incessantly stand on your head—
  Do you think, at your age, it is right?'

'In my youth,' Father William replied to his son,
  'I feared it might injure the brain;
But now that I'm perfectly sure I have none,
  Why, I do it again and again.'

'You are old,' said the youth, 'as I mentioned before,
    And have grown most uncommonly fat;
Yet you turned a back-somersault in at the door—
    Pray, what is the reason of that?'

'In my youth,' said the sage, as he shook his gray locks,
    'I kept all my limbs very supple
By the use of this ointment—one shilling the box—
    Allow me to sell you a couple?'

'You are old,' said the youth, 'and your jaws are too weak
    For anything tougher than suet;
Yet you finished the goose, with the bones and the beak—
    Pray how did you manage to do it?'

'In my youth,' said his father, 'I took to the law,
    And argued each case with my wife;
And the muscular strength, which it gave to my jaw,
    Has lasted the rest of my life.'

'You are old,' said the youth, 'one would hardly suppose
    That your eye was as steady as ever;
Yet you balanced an eel on the end of your nose—
    What made you so awfully clever?'

'I have answered three questions, and that is enough,'
    Said his father; 'don't give yourself airs.
Do you think I can listen all day to such stuff?
    Be off, or I'll kick you downstairs.'

The Snow-Storm

RALPH WALDO EMERSON

Announced by all the trumpets of the sky,
Arrives the snow, and, driving o'er the fields,
Seems nowhere to alight: the white air
Hides hills and woods, the river, and the heaven,
And veils the farm-house at the garden's end.
The sled and traveller stopped, the courier's feet
Delayed, all friends shut out, the housemates sit
Around the radiant fireplace, enclosed
In a tumultuous privacy of storm.

Come see the north wind's masonry.
Out of an unseen quarry evermore
Furnished with tile, the fierce artificer
Curves his white bastions with projected roof
Round every windward stake, or tree, or door.
Speeding, the myriad-handed, his wild work
So fanciful, so savage, nought cares he
For number or proportion. Mockingly,
On coop or kennel he hangs Parian wreaths;
A swan-like form invests the hidden thorn;
Fills up the farmer's lane from wall to wall,
Maugre the farmer's sighs; and at the gate
A tapering turret overtops the work.
And when his hours are numbered, and the world
Is all his own, retiring, as he were not,
Leaves, when the sun appears, astonished Art
To mimic in slow structures, stone by stone,
Built in an age, the mad wind's night-work,
The frolic architecture of the snow.

The Bitter Withy

ANONYMOUS

As it fell out on a Holy day
  The drops of rain did fall, did fall,
Our Saviour asked leave of His mother Mary
  If he might go play at ball.

'To play at ball my own dear Son,
  It's time You was going or gone,
But be sure let me hear no complaint of You
  At night when You do come home.'

It was upling scorn and downling scorn,
  Oh, there He met three jolly jerdins
Oh, there He asked the three jolly jerdins
  If they would go play at ball.

'Oh, we are lords' and ladies' sons,
  Born in bower or in hall,
And you are but some poor maid's child
  Born'd in an ox's stall.'

'If you are lords' and ladies' sons,
  Born'd in bower or in hall,
Then at the very last I'll make it appear
  That I am above you all.'

Our Saviour built a bridge with the beams of the sun,
  And over He gone, He gone He,
And after followed the three jolly jerdins,
  And drowned they were all three.

It was upling scorn and downling scorn
  The mothers of them did whoop and call,
Crying out, 'Mary mild, call back your Child,
  For ours are drowned all.'

Mary mild, Mary mild, called home her Child,
   And laid our Saviour across her knee,
And with a whole handful of bitter withy
   She gave Him slashes three.

Then He says to His mother, 'Oh! the withy,
               oh! the withy.
   The bitter withy that causes me to smart, to smart,
Oh! the withy it shall be the very first tree
   That perishes at the heart.'

Releasing a Migrant 'Yen' or Wild Goose

PO CHÜ-I

Translated by Arthur Waley

At Nine Rivers, in the tenth year, in winter—heavy snow;
The river-water covered with ice and the forests broken with
               their load.
The birds of the air, hungry and cold, went flying east and west;
And with them flew a migrant 'yen', loudly clamouring for food.

Among the snow it pecked for grass, and rested on the surface
               of the ice;
It tried with its wings to scale the sky, but its tired flight was slow.
The boys of the river spread a net and caught the bird as it flew.
They took it in their hands to the city-market and sold it
               there alive.
I that was once a man of the North am now an exile here;
Bird and man, in their different kind, are each strangers in
               the south.
And because the sight of an exiled bird wounded an exile's heart,
I paid your ransom and set you free, and you flew away to the
               clouds.

Yen, Yen, flying to the clouds, tell me, whither shall you go?
Of all things I bid you, do not fly to the land of the north-west.
In Huai-hsi there are rebel bands that have not been subdued;
And a thousand thousand armoured men have long been
                                        camped in war.
The official army and the rebel army have grown old in the
                                        opposite trenches;
The soldiers' rations have grown so small, they'll be glad of
                                        even you.
The brave boys, in their hungry plight, will shoot you and
                                        eat your flesh;
They will pluck from your body those long feathers and make
                                        them into arrow-wings!

A Fire in London, 1715

JOHN GAY

But hark! distress with screaming voice draws nigh'r,
And wakes the slumb'ring street with cries of fire.
At first a glowing red enwraps the skies,
And borne by winds the scatt'ring sparks arise;
From beam to beam the fierce contagion spreads:
The spiry flames now lift aloft their heads,
Through the burst sash a blazing deluge pours,
And splitting tiles descend in rattling showers.
Now with thick crowds th'enlighten'd pavement swarms,
The fireman sweats beneath his crooked arms,
A leathern casque his venturous head defends,
Boldly he climbs where thickest smoke ascends,
Moved by the mother's streaming eyes and prayers,
The helpless infant through the flame he bears,
With no less virtue, than through hostile fire
The Dardan hero bore his aged sire.

See forceful engines spout their levell'd streams,
To quench the blaze that runs along the beams;
The grappling hook plucks rafters from the walls,
And heaps on heaps the smoky ruin falls.
Blown by strong winds the fiery tempest roars,
Bears down new walls, and pours along the floors;
The Heavens are all ablaze, the face of night
Is covered with a sanguine dreadful light:
'Twas such a light involved thy towers, O Rome,
The dire presage of mighty Caesar's doom,
When the sun veiled in rust his mourning head,
And frightful prodigies the skies o'erspread.
Hark! the drum thunders! far, ye crowds, retire:
Behold, the ready match is tipt with fire,
The nitrous store is paid, the smutty train
With running blaze awakes the barrell'd grain;
Flames sudden wrap the walls; with sullen sound
The shatter'd pile sinks on the smoky ground.

Sourwood Mountain

ANONYMOUS

Chickens a crowing in Sourwood Mountain,
Hay diddy ump, diddy iddy um day.
Get your dogs and we'll all go a-hunting,
Hay diddy ump, diddy iddy um day.

Raccoon canter and 'possum trot,
Black cur wrestle with a hickory knot.

Bring your old dog, get your gun,
Kill some game and have a little fun.

Jaybird sitting on a hickory limb,
My six-foot rifle will sure get him.

Gather that game and at home I'll rack,
Got as much good meat as I can carry.

I got a gal in the head of the hollow
She won't come and I won't follow.

She sits up with old Si Hall,
Me and Jeff can't go there at all.

Some of these days before very long,
I'll get that girl and a-home I'll run.

New Hampshire

T. S. ELIOT

Children's voices in the orchard
Between the blossom- and the fruit-time:
Golden head, crimson head,
Between the green tip and the root.
Black wing, brown wing, hover over;
Twenty years and the spring is over;
To-day grieves, to-morrow grieves,
Cover me over, light-in-leaves;
Golden head, black wing,
Cling, swing,
Spring, sing,
Swing up into the apple-tree.

The Owl

EDWARD THOMAS

Downhill I came, hungry, and yet not starved;
Cold, yet had heat within me that was proof
Against the North wind; tired, yet so that rest
Had seemed the sweetest thing under a roof.

Then at the inn I had food, fire, and rest,
Knowing how hungry, cold, and tired was I.
All of the night was quite barred out except
An owl's cry, a most melancholy cry

Shaken out long and clear upon the hill,
No merry note, nor cause of merriment,
But one telling me plain what I escaped
And others could not, that night, as in I went.

And salted was my food, and my repose,
Salted and sobered, too, by the bird's voice
Speaking for all who lay under the stars,
Soldiers and poor, unable to rejoice.

A Ballad of Agincourt

MICHAEL DRAYTON

Fair stood the wind for France
When we our sails advance.
Nor now to prove our chance
  Longer will tarry;

But putting to the main,
At Caux, the mouth of Seine,
With all his martial train,
  Landed King Harry.

And taking many a fort,
Furnish'd in warlike sort,
Coming toward Agincourt
  In happy hour,
Skirmishing day by day
With those that stopp'd his way,
Where the French gen'ral lay
  With all his power:

Which, in his height of pride,
King Henry to deride,
His ransom to provide
  Unto him sending;
Which he neglects the while,
As from a nation vile,
Yet with an angry smile,
  Their fall portending;

And turning to his men,
Quoth our brave Henry then,
'Though they to one be ten,
  Be not amazèd:
Yet have we well begun;
Battles so bravely won
Have ever to the sun
  By fame been raisèd.

'And for myself (quoth he)
This my full rest shall be:
England ne'er mourn for me
  Nor more esteem me:

Victor I will remain
Or on this earth lie slain,
Never shall she sustain
    Loss to redeem me.

'Poitiers and Cressy tell,
When most their pride did swell,
Under our swords they fell:
    No less our skill is
Than when our grandsire great,
Claiming the regal seat,
By many a warlike feat
    Lopp'd the French lilies.'

The Duke of York so dread
The eager vaward led;
With the main Henry sped
    Among his henchmen.
Excester had the rear,
A braver man not there;
O lord, how hot they were
    On the false Frenchmen!

They now to fight are gone,
Armour on armour shone,
Drum unto drum did groan,
    To hear was wonder;
That with the cries they make
The very earth did shake;
Trumpet to trumpet spake,
    Thunder to thunder.

Well it thine age became,
O noble Erpingham,
Which didst the signal aim
    To our hid forces!

When from a meadow by,
Like a storm suddenly
The English archery
   Struck the French horses.

With Spanish yew so strong,
Arrows a cloth-yard long,
That like to serpents stung,
   Piercing the weather;
None from his fellow starts,
But playing manly parts,
And like true English hearts
   Stuck close together.

When down their bows they threw,
And forth their bilboes drew,
And on the French they flew,
   No man was tardy;
Arms were from shoulders sent,
Scalps to the teeth were rent,
Down the French peasants went—
   Our men were hardy.

This while our noble king,
His broadsword brandishing,
Down the French host did ding,
   As to o'erwhelm it;
And many a deep wound lent,
His arms with blood besprent,
And many a cruel dent
   Bruisèd his helmet.

Gloster, that duke so good,
Next of the royal blood,
For famous England stood,
   With his brave brother;

Clarence, in steel most bright,
Though but a maiden knight,
Yet in that furious fight
   Scarce such another.

Warwick in blood did wade,
Oxford the foe invade,
And cruel slaughter made
   Still as they ran up;
Suffolk his axe did ply,
Beaumont and Willoughby
Bare them right doughtily,
   Ferrers and Fanhope.

Upon Saint Crispin's Day
Fought was this noble fray,
Which fame did not delay
   To England to carry.
O when shall English men
With such acts fill a pen?
Or England breed again
   Such a King Harry?

Faith is a Fine Invention

EMILY DICKINSON

Faith is a fine invention
For gentlemen who see;
But microscopes are prudent
In an emergency!

Pied Beauty

GERARD MANLEY HOPKINS

Glory be to God for dappled things—
  For skies of couple-colour as a brinded cow;
    For rose-moles all in stipple upon trout that swim;
Fresh-firecoal chestnut-falls; finches' wings;
  Landscape plotted and pierced—fold, fallow, and plough;
    And áll trádes, their gear and tackle and trim.

All things counter, original, spare, strange;
  Whatever is fickle, freckled (who knows how?)
    With swift, slow; sweet, sour; adazzle, dim;
He fathers-forth whose beauty is past change:
                Praise him.

The Avondale Mine Disaster

ANONYMOUS

Good Christians all, both great and small,
I pray you lend an ear,
And listen with attention while
The truth I will declare;
When you hear this lamentation
'Twill cause you to weep and wail,
About the suffocation
In the mines of Avondale.

On the sixth day of September,
Eighteen sixty-nine,
Those miners all then got a call
To go to work in the mine;

But little did they think that day
That death would soon prevail
Before they would return again from
The mines of Avondale.

The women and their children,
Their hearts were filled with joy
To see their men go to their work
Likewise every boy;
But a dismal sight in broad daylight,
Soon made them turn pale,
When they saw the breaker burning
O'er the mines of Avondale.

From here and there and everywhere,
They gathered in a crowd,
Come tearing off their clothes and hair,
And crying out aloud—
'Get out our husbands and our sons,
Death he's going to steal
Their lives away without delay
In the mines of Avondale.'

But all in vain, there was no hope
One single soul to save,
For there is no second outlet
From the subterranean cave.
No pen can write the awful fright
And horror that prevailed,
Among those dying victims,
In the mines of Avondale.

A consultation then was held,
'Twas asked who'd volunteer
For to go down this dismal shaft
To seek their comrades dear;

Two Welshmen brave, without dismay,
And courage without fail,
Went down the shaft, without delay,
In the mines of Avondale.

When at the bottom they arrived,
And thought to make their way,
One of them died for want of air,
While the other in great dismay,
He gave a sign to hoist him up,
To tell the dreadful tale,
That all were lost forever
In the mines of Avondale.

Every effort then took place
To send down some fresh air;
The men that next went down again
They took of them good care;
And traversed through the chambers,
And this time did not fail
In finding those dead bodies
In the mines of Avondale.

Sixty-seven was the number
That in a heap were found.
It seemed that they were bewailing
Their fate underneath the ground;
They found the father with his son
Clasped in his arms so pale.
It was a heart-rending scene
In the mines of Avondale.

Now to conclude, and make an end,
Their number I'll pen down—
A hundred and ten of brave strong men
Were smothered underground;

They're in their graves till the last day,
Their widows may bewail,
And the orphans' cries they rend the skies
All around through Avondale!

Grasshoppers

JOHN CLARE

Grasshoppers go in many a thrumming spring
And now to stalks of tasselled sour-grass cling,
That shakes and swees awhile, but still keeps straight;
While arching oxeye doubles with his weight.
Next on the cat-tail grass with farther bound
He springs, that bends until they touch the ground.

The Horse

AUTHORISED VERSION OF THE BIBLE

Hast thou given the horse strength? Hast thou clothed his
    neck with thunder?
Canst thou make him afraid as a grasshopper?
The glory of his nostrils is terrible.
He paweth in the valley, and rejoiceth in his strength:
He goeth on to meet the armed men.
He mocketh at fear, and is not affrighted; neither turneth he
    back from the sword.
The quiver rattleth against him, the glittering spear and the
    shield.
He swalloweth the ground with fierceness and rage; neither
    believeth he that it is the sound of the trumpet.
He saith among the trumpets, Ha, ha; and he smelleth the battle
    far off; the thunder of the captains, and the shouting.

To a Louse:
On Seeing One On a Lady's Bonnet
At Church

ROBERT BURNS

Ha! whaur ye gaun, ye crowlin' ferlie?
Your impudence protects you sairly;
I canna say but ye strunt rarely,
    Owre gauze and lace;
Tho', faith! I fear ye dine but sparely
    On sic a place.

Ye ugly, creepin' blastit wonner,
Detested, shunn'd by saunt an' sinner,
How daur ye set your fit upon her—
    Sae fine a lady?
Gae somewhere else and seek your dinner
    On some poor body.

Swith! in some beggar's haffet squattle;
There ye may creep, and sprawl, and sprattle,
Wi' ither kindred, jumping cattle,
    In shoals and nations;
Whaur horn nor bane ne'er daur unsettle
    Your thick plantations.

Now haud you there, ye're out o' sight,
Below the fatt'rels, snug and tight;
Na, faith ye yet! ye'll no be right,
    Till ye've got on it—
The verra tapmost, tow'rin height
    O' Miss's bonnet.

My sooth! right bauld ye set your nose out,
As plump an' grey as ony groset:
O for some rank, mercurial rozet,
  Or fell, red smeddum,
I'd gie you sic a hearty dose o't,
  Wad dress your droddum.

I wad na been surpris'd to spy
You on an auld wife's flainen toy;
Or aiblins some bit duddie boy,
  On's wyliecoat;
But Miss's fine Lunardi! fye!
  How daur ye do't?

O Jeany, dinna toss your head,
An' set your beauties a' abread!
Ye little ken what cursed speed
  The blastie's makin:
Thae winks an' finger-ends, I dread,
  Are notice takin.

O wad some Power the giftie gie us
To see oursels as ithers see us!
It wad frae mony a blunder free us,
  An' foolish notion:
What airs in dress an' gait wad lea'e us,
  An' ev'n devotion!

Redemption

GEORGE HERBERT

Having been tenant long to a rich Lord,
 Not thriving, I resolved to be bold,
 And make a suit unto him, to afford
A new small-rented lease, and cancell th' old.

In heaven at his manour I him sought:
   They told me there, that he was lately gone
   About some land, which he had dearly bought
Long since on earth, to take possession.

I straight return'd, and knowing his great birth,
   Sought him accordingly in great resorts;
   In cities, theatres, gardens, parks, and courts:
At length I heard a ragged noise and mirth

Of theeves and murderers: there I him espied,
Who straight, *Your suit is granted*, said, and died.

Lady Isabel and the Elf Knight

ANONYMOUS

He followed her up and he followed her down,
He followed her to the room where she lay,
And she had not the power to flee from his arms,
Nor the tongue to answer Nay, Nay, Nay,
Nor the tongue to answer Nay.

She got on her pony, pony brown,
He got on the iron grey.
They rode till they came to the blue water sea
In the length of a long summer day.

Get down, get down, my pretty little Miss,
Get down, these words I say.
Here I've drownded nine kings' daughters,
And you the tenth shall be.

Pull off, pull off that fine silken gown,
And lie it on yonder stone,
For it cost your father too much money
For to rot in the salt sea foam.

Turn your face around and about,
Turn to the green leaves on the tree,
For I don't think as nice a gentleman as you
A naked lady should see.

She picked him up and she plunged him in,
She plunged him in the depths of the sea,
Lie there, lie there, you false-hearted soul,
In the place of poor me.

Hand me down your soft silk hand,
O hand it down to me,
O hand me down your soft silk hand,
And married we shall be.

She got on her pony, pony brown,
And she led her iron grey.
She rode till she came to her father's gate
'Twas just three hours till day.

My pretty little parrot, my pretty little parrot,
Don't tell no tales on me,
Your cage shall be made out of yellow beaten gold
And hung in the willow tree.

Here lie I, Martin Elginbrodde

ANONYMOUS

Here lie I, Martin Elginbrodde:
Ha'e mercy o' my soul, Lord God,
As I wad do, were I Lord God
And ye were Martin Elginbrodde.

Edward

ANONYMOUS

'How came this blood on your shirt-sleeve?
O dear love tell me.'
'It is the blood of the old grey horse,
That ploughed that field for me,
That ploughed that field for me.'

'It does look too pale for the old grey horse
That ploughed that field for thee.'
'It is the blood of the old grey hound,
That trac'd that fox for me.'

'It does look too pale for the old grey hound
That trac'd that fox for thee.'
'It is the blood of my brother-in-law,
That went away with me.'

And it's 'What did you fall out about?
O dear love tell me.'
'About a little bit of bush,
That would soon have made a tree.'

And it's 'What will you do now my love?
O dear love tell me.'
'I'll set my foot in yonder ship
And I'll sail across the sea.'

And it's 'When will you come back my love?
O dear love tell me.'
'When the sun sets in yonder sycamore tree
And that will never be,
And that will never be.'

Paradise

GEORGE HERBERT

I Blesse thee, Lord, because I GROW
Among thy trees, which in a ROW
To thee both fruit and order OW.

What open force, or hidden CHARM
Can blast my fruit, or bring me HARM,
While the inclosure is thine ARM?

Inclose me still for fear I START.
Be to me rather sharp and TART,
Then let me want thy hand & ART.

When thou dost greater judgements SPARE,
And with thy knife but prune and PARE,
Ev'n fruitfull trees more fruitfull ARE.

Such sharpnes shows the sweetest FREND:
Such cuttings rather heal than REND:
And such beginnings touch their END.

Chinese Song of Courtship

ANONYMOUS
Translated by Arthur Waley

If along the highroad
I caught hold of your sleeve,
Do not hate me;
Old ways take time to overcome.

84

If along the highroad
I caught hold of your hand
Do not be angry with me;
Friendship takes time to overcome.

Hope

GEORGE HERBERT

I gave to Hope a watch of mine: but he
                     An anchor gave to me.
Then an old prayer-book I did present:
                     And he an optick sent.
With that I gave a viall full of tears:
                     But he a few green eares:
Ah Loyterer! I'le no more, no more I'le bring:
                     I did expect a ring.

I know some Lonely Houses off the Road

EMILY DICKINSON

I know some lonely houses off the road
A robber'd like the look of,—
Wooden barred,
And windows hanging low,
Inviting to
A portico,

Where two could creep:
One hand the tools,
The other peep
To make sure all's asleep.
Old-fashioned eyes,
Not easy to surprise!

How orderly the kitchen'd look by night,
With just a clock,—
But they could gag the tick,
And mice won't bark;
And so the walls don't tell,
None will.

A pair of spectacles ajar just stir—
An almanac's aware.
Was it the mat winked,
Or a nervous star?
The moon slides down the stair
To see who's there.

There's plunder,—where?
Tankard, or spoon,
Earring, or stone,
A watch, some ancient brooch
To match the grandmamma,
Staid sleeping there.

Day rattles, too,
Stealth's slow;
The sun has got as far
As the third sycamore.
Screams chanticleer,
'Who's there?'

And echoes, trains away,
Sneer—'Where?'
While the old couple, just astir,
Think that the sunrise left the door ajar!

Life

GEORGE HERBERT

I made a posie, while the day ran by:
Here will I smell my remnant out, and tie
My life within this band.
But time did becken to the flowers, and they
By noon most cunningly did steal away,
And wither'd in my hand.

My hand was next to them, and then my heart:
I took, without more thinking, in good part
Times gentle admonition:
Who did so sweetly deaths sad taste convey,
Making my minde to smell my fatall day:
Yet sugring the suspicion.

Farewell deare flowers, sweetly your time ye spent,
Fit, while ye liv'd, for smell or ornament,
And after death for cures:
I follow straight without complaints or grief,
Since if my scent be good, I care not, if
It be as short as yours.

The Bullwhacker

ANONYMOUS

I'm a lonely bullwhacker
On the Red Cloud line.
I kin lick any son-of-a-gun
Tries to yoke an ox of mine.

An' ef I kin catch him,
You bet I will or try,
I'll lick him with an oxbow,
Root, hog, or die.

It's out on the trail
With a dern heavy load,
With a contrairy team
An' a muddy old road.
You may whip, you may holler,
You may cuss on the sly,
An' whack the cattle on, boys,
Root, hog, or die.

It's out on the trail,
These sights to be seen:
The ant'lope, the buffalo,
The prairie so green.
The ant'lope, the buffalo,
The rabbit jump so high,
So whack the cattle on, boys,
Root, hog, or die.

It's every day at twelve,
There's somethin' fer to do,
An' if it's nothin' else
There's a pony to shoe.
I'll throw down that pony
An' still make him lie.
Little pig, big pig,
Root, hog, or die.

Now p'raps you'd like to know
What we have to eat:
A little bit of bread
An' a little dirty meat,

A little black coffee
An' whiskey on the sly,
So whack the cattle on, boys,
Root, hog, or die.

There's hard times on Bitter Creek,
That never kin be beat.
It was root, hog, or die
Under every wagon sheet.
We cleaned up the Injuns,
Drank all the alkali,
An' we whacked the cattle on, boys,
Root, hog, or die.

A Bushman's Song

A.B.PATERSON

I'm travelling down the Castlereagh, and I'm a station-hand,
I'm handy with the ropin' pole, I'm handy with the brand,
And I can ride a rowdy colt, or swing the axe all day,
But there's no demand for a station-hand along the Castlereagh.

So it's shift, boys, shift, for there isn't the slightest doubt
That we've got to make a shift to the stations further out,
With the pack-horse runnin' after, for he follows like a dog,
We must strike across the country at the old jig-jog.

This old black horse I'm riding—if you'll notice what's his brand,
He wears the crooked R, you see—none better in the land.
He takes a lot of beatin', and the other day we tried,
For a bit of a joke, with a racing bloke, for twenty pound a side.

It was shift, boys, shift, for there wasn't the slightest doubt
That I had to make him shift, for the money was nearly out,
But he cantered home a winner, with the other one at the flog—
He's a red-hot sort to pick up with his old jig-jog.

I asked a cove for shearin' once along the Marthaguy:
'We shear non-union here', says he. 'I call it scab', says I.
I looked along the shearin' floor before I turned to go—
There were eight or ten dashed Chinamen a-shearin' in a row.

It was shift, boys, shift, for there wasn't the slightest doubt
It was time to make a shift with the leprosy about.
So I saddled up my horses, and I whistled to my dog,
And I left his scabby station at the old jig-jog.

I went to Illawarra, where my brother's got a farm;
He has to ask his landlord's leave before he lifts his arm:
The landlord owns the country-side—man, woman, dog and cat,
They haven't the cheek to dare to speak without they touch their h

It was shift, boys, shift, for there wasn't the slightest doubt
Their little landlord god an' I would soon have fallen out;
Was I to touch my hat to him?—was I his bloomin dog?
So I makes for up the country at the old jig-jog.

But it's time that I was movin', I've a mighty way to go
Till I drink artesian water from a thousand feet below;
Till I meet the overlanders with the cattle comin' down—
And I'll work a while till I make a pile, then have a spree in town.

So it's shift, boys, shift, for there isn't the slightest doubt
We've got to make a shift to the stations further out:
The pack-horse runs behind us, for he follows like a dog,
And we cross a lot of country at the old jig-jog.

Nottamun Town

ANONYMOUS

In Nottamun Town not a soul would look up,
Not a soul would look up, not a soul would look down
To tell me the way to Nottamun Town.

I rode a big horse that was called a grey mare,
Grey mane and tail and grey stripes down his back,
There weren't a hair on him but what was called black.

She stood so still, she threw me to the dirt,
She tore my hide and bruised my shirt.
From stirrup to saddle I mounted again,
And on my ten toes I rode over the plain.

I met the king and the queen and a company of men
A-walking behind and riding before;
A stark naked drummer came marching along
With his hands in his bosom always beating his drum.

I brought me a quart to drive gladness away,
To stifle the dirt for it rained the whole day.

Sat down on a hot, cold frozen stone,
Ten thousand stood round me, yet I was alone.
I took my heart in my hand to keep my head warm.
Ten thousand got drowned that never was born.

On Andrew Turner

ROBERT BURNS

In se'enteen hunder 'n forty-nine,
The deil gat stuff to mak a swine,
   An' coost it in a corner;
But wilily he chang'd his plan,
An' shap'd it something like a man,
   An' ca'd it Andrew Turner.

The Pool in the Rock

WALTER DE LA MARE

In this water, clear as air,
Lurks a lobster in its lair.
Rock-bound weed sways out and in,
Coral-red, and bottle-green.
Wondrous pale anemones
Stir like flowers in a breeze:
Fluted scallop, whelk in shell,
And the prowling mackerel.
Winged with snow the sea-mews ride
The brine-keen wind; and far and wide
Sounds on the hollow thunder of the tide.

Kubla Khan: or, A Vision in a Dream

SAMUEL TAYLOR COLERIDGE

In Xanadu did Kubla Khan
   A stately pleasure-dome decree:
Where Alph, the sacred river, ran
Through caverns measureless to man
   Down to a sunless sea.
So twice five miles of fertile ground
With walls and towers were girdled round:
And there were gardens bright with sinuous rills,
Where blossomed many an incense-bearing tree;
And here were forests ancient as the hills,
Enfolding sunny spots of greenery.
But oh! that deep romantic chasm which slanted
Down the green hill athwart a cedarn cover!
A savage place! as holy and enchanted

92

As e'er beneath a waning moon was haunted
By woman wailing for her demon lover!
And from this chasm, with ceaseless turmoil seething,
As if this earth in fast thick pants were breathing,
A mighty fountain momently was forced:
Amid whose swift half-intermitted burst
Huge fragments vaulted like rebounding hail,
Or chaffy grain beneath the thresher's flail:
And 'mid these dancing rocks at once and ever
It flung up momently the sacred river.
Five miles meandering with a mazy motion
Through wood and dale the sacred river ran,
Then reached the caverns measureless to man,
And sank in tumult to a lifeless ocean:
And 'mid this tumult Kubla heard from far
Ancestral voices prophesying war!
   The shadow of the dome of pleasure
   Floated midway on the waves;
   Where was heard the mingled measure
   From the fountain and the caves.
It was a miracle of rare device,
A sunny pleasure-dome with caves of ice!

   A damsel with a dulcimer
   In a vision once I saw:
   It was an Abyssinian maid,
   And on a dulcimer she play'd,
   Singing of Mount Abora,
   Could I revive within me
   Her symphony and song,
   To such a deep delight 'twould win me,
That with music loud and long,
I would build that dome in air,
That sunny dome! those caves of ice!
And all who heard should see them there

And all should cry, Beware! Beware!
His flashing eyes, his floating hair!
Weave a circle round him thrice,
And close your eyes with holy dread,
For he on honey-dew hath fed,
And drunk the milk of Paradise.

The Song of Wandering Aengus

W. B. YEATS

I went out to the hazel wood,
Because a fire was in my head,
And cut and peeled a hazel wand,
And hooked a berry to a thread;
And when white moths were on the wing,
And moth-like stars were flickering out,
I dropped the berry in a stream
And caught a little silver trout.

When I had laid it on the floor
I went to blow the fire aflame,
But something rustled on the floor,
And some one called me by my name:
It had become a glimmering girl
With apple blossom in her hair
Who called me by my name and ran
And faded through the brightening air.

Though I am old with wandering
Through hollow lands and hilly lands,
I will find out where she has gone,
And kiss her lips and take her hands;

And walk among long dappled grass,
And pluck till time and times are done
The silver apples of the moon,
The golden apples of the sun.

The Garden of Love

WILLIAM BLAKE

I went to the garden of love,
And saw what I never had seen:
A Chapel was built in the midst,
Where I used to play on the green.

And the gates of this Chapel were shut,
And 'Thou shalt not' writ over the door;
So I turn'd to the Garden of Love
That so many sweet flowers bore;

And I saw it was filled with graves,
And tomb-stones where flowers should be;
And Priests in black gowns were walking their rounds,
And binding with briars my joys & desires.

Jesu

GEORGE HERBERT

Jesu is in my heart, his sacred name
Is deeply carved there: but th'other week
A great affliction broke the little frame,
Ev'n all to pieces: which I went to seek:

And first I found the corner, where was *J*,
After, where *ES*, and next where *U* was graved.
When I had got these parcels, instantly
I sat me down to spell them, and perceived
That to my broken heart he was *I ease you*,
And to my whole is *JESU*.

John Hardy

ANONYMOUS

John Hardy was a brave and a desperate boy,
Said he carried two guns every day.
He shot him a man in the Shawnee camp,
And I seen John gettin' away, poor boy!
And I seen John Hardy gettin' away.

John Hardy had a little lovin' wife,
And children he had three,
But he cared no more for his wife and babes,
Than he cared for the rocks in the sea, poor boy!
Than he cared for the rocks in the sea.

John Hardy was a-standin' by the dark sea bar,
He was unconcerned in the game,
Up stepped a yaller girl with twenty dollars in her hand,
Said: 'Deal John Hardy in the game, poor boy!'
Said: 'Deal John Hardy in the game.'

John Hardy stepped up with the money in his hand,
Sayin': 'I have money for to play,
And the one who wins this yaller girl's dough,
I have powder to blow him away, poor boy!
I have powder to blow him away.'

The cards was dealt and the money on the board.
Dave Campbell won that twenty dollar bill.
John Hardy drew his pistol and took sure aim and fired,
And he caused Dave Campbell's brains to spill, poor boy!
And he caused Dave Campbell's brains to spill.

John Hardy had twelve mile to go
And six of them he ran.
He ran, he came to the river bank,
Then he fell on his bosom and he swam, poor boy!
Then he fell on his bosom and he swam.

John Hardy went to this big long town,
And he thought he was out of the way.
Up stepped a marshal and took him by the hand,
Says: 'John Hardy, come and go with me, poor boy!'
Says: 'John Hardy, come and go with me.'

John Hardy's wife was dressed in blue.
She came for to go his bail.
No bail was allowed for murderin' a man,
So they put John Hardy back in jail, poor boy!
So they put John Hardy back in jail.

John Hardy stood in the middle of his cell,
And the tears run down his eyes,
Says: 'I've been the death of many a man
And now I am ready for to die, poor boy!
And now I am ready for to die.

I've been to the East, I've been to the West,
I've travelled this wide world round.
I've been down to the river and I've been baptized,
So take me to the hangin' ground, poor boy!
So take me to the hangin' ground.'

The Orchard

WALTER DE LA MARE

Lapped in the light and heat of noon,
I saw an orchard—glorious
With countless, cup-shaped, coloured flowers
Of intertwined convolvulus.

At sun-down, I came back again—
Faint shadows in the twilight wan;
A hundred aging apple trees;
But they?—all gone.

Snake into Woman

JOHN KEATS

Left to herself, the serpent now began
To change; her elfin blood in madness ran,
Her mouth foam'd, and the grass, therewith besprent,
Wither'd at dew so sweet and virulent;
Her eyes in torture fix'd, and anguish drear,
Hot, glaz'd, and wide, with lid-lashes all sear,
Flash'd phosphor and sharp sparks, without one cooling tear.
The colours all inflam'd throughout her train,
She writh'd about, convuls'd with scarlet pain:
A deep volcanian yellow took the place
Of all her milder-mooned body's grace;
And, as the lava ravishes the mead,
Spoilt all her silver, and golden brede;
Made gloom of all her frecklings, streaks and bars,
Eclips'd her crescents, and lick'd up her stars:
So that, in moments few, she was undrest
Of all her sapphires, greens, and amethyst,

And rubious-argent: of all these bereft,
Nothing but pain and ugliness were left.
Still shone her crown; that vanish'd, also she
Melted and disappear'd as suddenly;
And in the air, her new voice luting soft,
Cried, 'Lycius! gentle Lycius!'—Borne aloft
With the bright mists about the mountains hoar
These words dissolv'd Crete's forests heard no more.

The World

GEORGE HERBERT

Love built a stately house; where *Fortune* came,
And spinning fancies, she was heard to say,
That her fine cobwebs did support the frame,
Whereas they were supported by the same:
But *Wisdome* quickly swept them all away.

Then *Pleasure* came, who liking not the fashion,
Began to make *Balconies, Terraces,*
Till she had weakened all by alteration:
But rev'rend *laws,* and many a *proclamation*
Reformed all at length with menaces.

Then enter'd *Sinne,* and with that Sycamore,
Whose leaves first sheltered man from drought and dew,
Working and winding slily evermore,
The inward walls and summers cleft and tore:
But *Grace* shor'd these, and cut that as it grew.

Then *Sinne* combin'd with *Death* in a firm band
To rase the building to the very floore:
Which they effected, none could them withstand,
But *Love* and *Grace* took *Glorie* by the hand,
And built a braver Palace than before.

99

Love without Hope

ROBERT GRAVES

Love without hope, as when the young bird-catcher
Swept off his tall hat to the Squire's own daughter,
So let the imprisoned larks escape and fly
Singing about her head, as she rode by.

The Poor People's Common Land

GEORGE CRABBE

Lo! where the heath, with withering brake grown o'er,
Lends the light turf that warms the neighbouring poor;
From thence a length of burning sand appears,
Where the thin harvest waves its withered ears;
Rank weeds, that every art and care defy,
Reign o'er the land, and rob the blighted rye:
There thistles stretch their prickly arms afar,
And to the ragged infant threaten war;
There poppies nodding, mock the hope of toil;
There the blue bugloss paints the sterile soil;
Hardy and high, above the slender sheaf,
The slimy mallow waves her silky leaf;
O'er the young shoot the charlock throws a shade,
And clasping tares cling round the sickly blade;
With mingled tints the rocky coasts abound,
And a sad splendour vainly shines around.

Marching (as seen from the Left File)

ISAAC ROSENBERG

My eyes catch ruddy necks
Sturdily pressed back—
All a red brick moving glint.
Like flaming pendulums, hands
Swing across the khaki—
Mustard-coloured khaki—
To the automatic feet.

We husband the ancient glory
In these bared necks and hands.
Not broke is the forge of Mars;
But a subtler brain beats iron
To shoe the hoofs of death
(Who paws dynamic air now).
Blind fingers loose an iron cloud
To rain immortal darkness
On strong eyes.

A Glimpse into the Great Beyond

EDGELL RICKWORD

Sir Arthur Conan Doyle is reported to have held several conversations, since his decease, with Mr Hannen Swaffer, a Fleet Street journalist.

Now that Sir Arthur has the run
of all the pleasures Space can offer,
might we conclude they're not much fun
since he comes back to talk to Swaffer?

Old John Brown's Body

ANONYMOUS

Old John Brown's body lies a-mould'ring in the grave,
While weep the sons of bondage whom he ventur'd all to save;
But though he lost his life in struggling for the slave,
   His soul is marching on.
Oh, glory hallelujah, glory, glory hallelujah.

John Brown was a hero, undaunted true and brave,
Kansas knew his valour when he fought her rights to save;
And now though the grass grows green above his grave,
   His soul is marching on.

He captur'd Harper's Ferry with his nineteen men so few,
And he frighten'd 'Old Virginny' till she trembled thro' and thro'
They hung him for a traitor, themselves a traitor crew.
   But his soul is marching on.

John Brown was John the Baptist for the Christ we are to see,
Christ who of the bondman shall the liberator be,
And soon throughout the Sunny South, the slaves shall be all free,
   For his soul is marching on.

The conflict that he heralded he looks from heav'n to view,
On the army of the Union, with its flag, red, white, and blue,
And heav'n shall ring with anthems o'er the deeds they mean to do,
   For his soul is marching on.

Soldiers of freedom then strike while strike you may,
The death-blow of oppression is a better time and way,
For the dawn of Old John Brown has bright'ned into day,
   And his soul is marching on.

Springfield Mountain

ANONYMOUS

On Springfield Mountain there did dwell
A lovely lad, I knew him well;
When he became twenty-one,
The grandest rascal under the sun,

And a rumble, bumble skiddy I gum,
And a rose I ling cum loo.

One morning John he did go
Down in the meadow for to mow.
He'd scarcely mowed half round the field
When a venomous serpent bit him on the heel.

John picked that snake up in his hand
And carried it straight to Molly Anne.
Says John to Moll: Just look and see
What a venomous serpent has bitten me.

Says Moll to John: Why did you go
Down in the meadow for to mow?
Says John to Moll: I thought you knowed
That daddy's hay it must be mowed.

Poor John he died, gave up the ghost,
And went to join the heavenly host.
He cried, he cried, as on he went:
Confound that devil of a ser-pi-ent.

Words

EDWARD THOMAS

Out of us all
That make rhymes,
Will you choose
Sometimes—
As the winds use
A crack in a wall
Or a drain,
Their joy or their pain
To whistle through—
Choose me,
You English words?

I know you:
You are light as dreams,
Tough as oak,
Precious as gold,
As poppies and corn,
Or an old cloak:
Sweet as our birds
To the ear,
As the burnet rose
In the heat
Of Midsummer:
Strange as the races
Of dead and unborn:
Strange and sweet
Equally,
And familiar,
To the eye,
As the dearest faces
That a man knows,

And as lost homes are:
But though older far
Than oldest yew,—
As our hills are, old,—
Worn anew
Again and again:
Young as our streams
After rain:
And as dear
As the earth which you prove
That we love.

Make me content
With some sweetness
From Wales
Whose nightingales
Have no wings,—
From Wiltshire and Kent
And Herefordshire,
And the villages there,—
From the names, and the things
No less.
Let me sometimes dance
With you,
Or climb
Or stand perchance
In ecstasy,
Fixed and free
In a rhyme,
As poets do.

In a Wood (from 'The Woodlanders')

THOMAS HARDY

Pale beech and pine so blue,
  Set in one clay,
Bough to bough cannot you
  Live out your day?
When the rains skim and skip,
Why mar sweet comradeship,
Blighting with poison-drip
  Neighbourly spray?

Heart-halt and spirit-lame,
  City-opprest,
Unto this wood I came
  As to a nest;
Dreaming that sylvan peace
Offered the harrowed ease—
Nature a soft release
  From men's unrest.

But, having entered in,
  Great growths and small
Show them to men akin—
  Combatants all!
Sycamore shoulders oak,
Bines the slim sapling yoke,
Ivy-spun halters choke
  Elms stout and tall.

Touches from ash, O wych,
  Sting you like scorn!
You, too, brave hollies, twitch
  Sidelong from thorn.

Even the rank poplars bear
Lothly a rival's air,
Cankering in black despair
　　If overborne.

Since, then, no grace I find
　　Taught me of trees,
Turn I back to my kind,
　　Worthy as these.
There at least smiles abound,
There discourse trills around,
There, now and then, are found
　　Life-loyalties.

London Nights

SAMUEL JOHNSON

Prepare for death if here at night you roam,
And sign your will before you sup from home.
　　Some fiery fop, with new commission vain,
Who sleeps on brambles till he kills his man;
Some frolic drunkard, reeling from a feast,
Provokes a broil, and stabs you for a jest...
　　In vain, these dangers past, your doors you close,
And hope the balmy blessings of repose;
Cruel with guilt, and daring with despair,
The midnight murd'rer bursts the faithless bar;
Invades the sacred hour of silent rest,
And leaves, unseen, a dagger in your breast.

The Red Cockatoo

PO CHÜ-I

Translated by Arthur Waley

Sent as a present from Annam—
A red cockatoo.
Coloured like the peach-tree blossom,
Speaking with the speech of men,
And they did to it what is always done
To the learned and eloquent.
They took a cage with stout bars
And shut it up inside.

A Cat

EDWARD THOMAS

She had a name among the children;
But no one loved though someone owned
Her, locked her out of doors at bedtime
And had her kittens duly drowned.

In Spring, nevertheless, this cat
Ate blackbirds, thrushes, nightingales,
And birds of bright voice and plume and flight,
As well as scrape from neighbours' pails.

I loathed and hated her for this;
One speckle on a thrush's breast
Was worth a million such; and yet
She lived long, till God gave her rest.

The Ground Hog

ANONYMOUS

Shoulder up your gun and call your dog,
Shoulder up your gun and call your dog,
Away to the woods to catch a ground hog.
  Ground hog.

Two in the cleft and one in the log,
See'd his nose, Lord, I thought I knew it was a hog.
  Ground hog.

Children all around, they screamed and cried,
They love a ground hog stewed and fried.
  Ground hog.

Yonder comes Fate with a very long pole,
To run these ground hogs to their hole.
  Ground hog.

I skin his hide and I tan his hide.
Lord, Lord, Mamma, what a ground hog hide.
  Ground hog.

I took him to the house and I whetted up my knife;
He's good meat, I says to my wife.
  Ground hog.

Yonder comes Sally with a snigger and a grin,
Ground hog grease all over her chin.
  Ground hog.

Description of a Thunderstorm

JOHN CLARE

Slow boiling up, on the horizon's brim,
Huge clouds arise, mountainous, dark and grim,
Sluggish and slow upon the air they ride,
As pitch-black ships o'er the blue ocean glide;
Curling and hovering o'er the gloomy south,
As curls the sulphur from the cannon's mouth.
More grisly in the sun the tempest comes,
And through the wood with threatened vengeance hums,
Hissing more loud and loud among the trees:
The frightened wild-wind trembles to a breeze,
Just turns the leaf in terrifying sighs,
Bows to the spirit of the storm, and dies.
In wild pulsations beats the heart of fear,
At the low rumbling thunder creeping near,
Like as I've heard the river's flood, confined
Thro' the gulled locks, hangs grumbling on the wind.
The poplar leaf now resteth on its tree;
And the mill-sail, once twirling rapidly,
Lagging and lagging till breeze had dropt,
Abruptly now in hesitation stopt.
The very cattle gaze upon the gloom,
And seemly dread the threatened fate to come.
The little birds sit mute within the bush,
And nature's very breath is stopt and hush.
The shepherd leaves his unprotected flock,
And flies for shelter in some scooping rock;
There hides in fear from the dread boding wrath,
Lest rocks should tremble when it sallies forth,
And that Almighty Power, that bids it roar,
Hath seal'd the doom when time shall be no more.
The cotter's family cringe round the hearth,

Where all is sadden'd but the cricket's mirth;
The boys through fear in soot-black corner push,
And 'tween their father's knees for safety crush;
Each leaves his plaything on the brick-barr' floor,
The idle top and ball can please no more,
And oft above the wheel's unceasing thrum
The murmur's heard to whisper—'Is it come?'
The clouds more dismal darken on the eye,
More huge, more fearful, and of deeper dye;
And, as unable to light up the gloom,
The sun drops sinking in its bulging tomb.
Now as one glizes skyward with affright,
Short vivid lightnings catch upon the sight;
While like to rumbling armies, as it were,
Th' approaching thunder mutters on the ear,
And still keeps creeping on more loud and loud,
And stronger lightnings splinter through the cloud.
An awe-struck monument of hope and fear,
Mute expectation waits the terror near,
That dreadful clap, that terminates suspense,
When ruin meets us or is banish'd hence.
The signal's giv'n in that explosive flash—
One moment's pause amid the clouds hell-black,
And then the red fire-bolt and horrid crash:
Almighty, what a shock!—the jostled wrack
Of nature seems in mingled ruins done;
Astounded echo rives the terrors back,
And tingles on the ear a dying swoon.
Flash, peal, and flash still rend the melting cloud;
All nature seems to sign her race is o'er,
And as she shrinks 'neath chaos' dismal shroud,
Gives meek consent that suns shall shine no more.
Where is the sinner now, with careless eye,
Will look, and say that all is chance's whim;
When hell e'en trembles at God's majesty,

And sullen owns that naught can equal Him?
But clouds now melt like mercy into tears,
And nature's Lord His wrath in kindness stops:
Each trembling cotter now delighted hears
The rain fall down in heavy-pattering drops.
The sun 'gins tremble through the cloud again,
And a slow murmur wakes the delug'd plain;
A number of thanksgiving, mix'd with fear,
For God's great power and our deliverance here.

Spring Comes

JOHN CLARE

Spring comes and it is May. White as are sheets,
　Each orchard shines beside its little town.
Children at every bush a posy meets,
　Bluebells and primroses—wandering up and down
　To hunt bird's nests and flowers a stone's throw
　　　　　　　　　　　　　　　　from the town,
And hear the blackbirds in the coppice sing.
　Green spots appear, like doubling a book down
To find the place agen; and strange birds sing
We have no name for in the burst of spring.

The sparrow comes and chelps about the slates
　And pops into her hole beneath the eaves,
While the cock pigeon amorously awaits
　The hen, on barn ridge cooing, and then leaves
　With crop all ruffled: where the sower heaves
The hopper at his side, his beans to sow,
　There he with timid courage harmless thieves,
And whirls around the teams, and then drops low,
While plops the sudden gun, and great the overthrow.

And in the maple bush, there hides the stile,
  And then the gate the hawthorn stands before—
Till close upon't you cannot see't the while;
  'Tis like to ivy creeping o'er a door,
  And green as spring, nor gap is seen before.
And still the path leads on, till 'neath your hand
  The gate waits to be opened, and then claps; the sower
Scatters the seeds of spring beneath his hand—
And then the footpath tracks the elting land.

Tall grows the nettle by the hedgeway side,
  And by the old barn and they shade the wall,
In sunshine nodding to the angry tide
  Of winds that winnows by: these one and all
  Make up the harmony of spring, and all
That passes feels a sudden love for flowers,
  They look so green; and when the soft showers fall
They grow so fast. Dock, burdocks, henbane, all,
Who loves not wild flowers by the old stone wall?

I love the little pond to meet at spring
  When frogs and toads are croaking round its brink,
When blackbirds' yellow bills 'gin first to sing
  And green woodpecker rotten trees to clink.
  I love to see the cattle muse and drink
And water crinkle to the rude March winds:
  While two ash dotterels flourish on its brink,
Bearing key-bunches children run to find—
And water-buttercups they're forced to leave behind.

The red-bagged bee on never-weary wing
  Pipes his small trumpet round the early flowers,
And the white nettles by the hedge in spring
  Hears his low music all the sunny hours,
  Till clouds come on and leave the falling showers.

Herald of spring and music of wild blooms,
    It seems the minstrel of spring's early flowers:
On banks where the red nettle flowers it comes,
And there all the long sunny morning hums.

Bluebells, how beautiful and bright they look,
    Bowed o'er green moss and pearled in morning dew,
Shedding a shower of pearls as soon as shook:
    In every wood-hedge gap they're shining through,
    Smelling of spring and beautifully blue.
Childhood and spring, how beautifully dwells
    Their memories in the woods we now walk through!
Oh, balmy days of spring in whitethorn dells,
How beautiful are woods and their bluebells!

Still I complain

EDWARD TAYLOR

I John II. 21 : And he is the propitiation for our sins ; and not for ours only, but also for the sins of the whole world.

Still I complain; I am complaining still.
    O woe is me! Was ever Heart like mine?
A Sty of Filth, a Trough of Washing-Swill,
    A Dunghill Pit, a Puddle of mere Slime,
    A Nest of Vipers, Hive of Hornets-stings,
    A Bag of Poyson, Civit-Box of Sins.

Was ever Heart like mine? So bad? black? vile?
    Is any Divell blacker? Or can Hell
Produce its match? It is the very soile
    Where Satan reads his charms and sets his spell;
    His Bowling Ally where he sheers his fleece
    At Nine Pins, Nine Holes, Morrice, Fox and Geese.

His Palace Garden where his courtiers walke;
  His Jewells cabbinet. Here his caball
Do sham it and truss up their Privie talk
  In Fardells of Consults and bundles all.
  His shambles and his Butchers stalls herein.
  It is the Fuddling Schoole of every sin.

Was ever Heart like mine? Pride, Passion fell,
  Ath'ism, Blasphemy pot, pipe it, dance,
Play Barlybreaks, and at Last Couple in Hell:
  At Cudgells, Kit-Cat, Cards and Dice here prance:
  At Noddy, Ruff-and-Trump, Jink, Post and Pare,
  Put, One-and-thirty, and such other ware.

Grace shuffled is away; Patience oft sticks
  Too soon, or draws itselfe out, and's out put.
Faith's over-trumpt, and oft doth lose her tricks.
  Repentance's chalkt up Noddy, and out shut.
  They Post and Pare off Grace thus, and its shine.
  Alas! alas! was ever Heart like mine?

Lucy

WILLIAM WORDSWORTH

Strange fits of passion have I known:
And I will dare to tell,
But in the Lover's ear alone,
What once to me befel.

When she I loved looked every day
Fresh as a rose in June,
I to her cottage bent my way,
Beneath an evening moon.

Upon the moon I fixed my eye,
All over the wide lea;
With quickening pace my horse drew nigh
Those paths so dear to me.

And now we reached the orchard-plot;
And, as we climbed the hill,
The sinking moon to Lucy's cot
Came near, and nearer still.

In one of those sweet dreams I slept,
Kind Nature's gentlest boon!
And all the while my eyes I kept
On the descending moon.

My horse moved on; hoof after hoof
He raised, and never stopped:
When down behind the cottage roof,
At once, the bright moon dropped.

What fond and wayward thoughts will slide
Into a Lover's head!
'O mercy!' to myself I cried,
'If Lucy should be dead!'

Return from Battle

ANONYMOUS CHINESE POET

Translated by Arthur Waley

WIFE: Tall grows that pear-tree,
       Its fruit so fair to see.
       The King's business never ends;
       Day in, day out it claims us.

CHORUS: In spring-time, on a day so sunny—
       Yet your heart is full of grief?
       The soldiers have leave!

WIFE: Tall grows that pear-tree,
       Its leaves so thick.
       The King's business never ends;
       My heart is sick and sad.
CHORUS: Every plant and tree so leafy,
       Yet your heart is sad?
       The soldiers are coming home!

SOLDIER: I climb that northern hill
       To pluck the boxthorn.
       The King's business never ends;
       What will become of my father, my mother?
CHORUS: Their wicked chariots drag painfully along,
       Their horses are tired out.
       But the soldiers have far to go.

WIFE: If he were not expected and did not come
       My heart would still be sad.
       But he named a day, and that day is passed,
       So that my torment is great indeed.
CHORUS: The tortoise and the yarrow stalks agree;
       Both tell glad news.
       Your soldier is close at hand.

The Cat and the Moon

W. B. YEATS

The cat went here and there
And the moon spun round like a top,
And the nearest kin of the moon,
The creeping cat, looked up.
Black Minnaloushe stared at the moon,
For, wander and wail as he would
The pure cold light in the sky
Troubled his animal blood.

Minnaloushe runs in the grass
Lifting his delicate feet.
Do you dance, Minnaloushe, do you dance?
When two close kindred meet,
What better than call a dance?
Maybe the moon may learn,
Tired of that courtly fashion,
A new dance turn.
Minnaloushe creeps through the grass
From moonlit place to place,
The sacred moon overhead
Has taken a new phase.
Does Minnaloushe know that his pupils
Will pass from change to change,
And that from round to crescent,
From crescent to round they range?
Minnaloushe creeps through the grass
Alone, important and wise,
And lifts to the changing moon
His changing eyes.

The Cuckoo

ANONYMOUS

The cuckoo is a pretty bird,
She singeth as she flies.
She bringeth us good tidings,
She telleth us no lies.
She sucketh of sweet flowers
To keep her throttle clear,
And every time she singeth
Cuckoo! Cuckoo! Cuckoo!
The summer draweth near.

Come all you pretty maidens
Wherever you be
Don't settle your mind on
A sycamore tree
For the leaves they'll but wither
And the branches will die
And you'll be forsaken,
You not know for why.

And when I have found out
My joy and delight
I'll be constant unto him
By day and by night
I will always prove constant
As a true turtle dove
And I never will in no time
Prove false to my love.

A Sheep Fair

THOMAS HARDY

The day arrives of the autumn fair,
   And torrents fall,
Though sheep in throngs are gathered there,
   Ten thousand all,
Sodden with hurdles round them reared:
   And, lot by lot, the pens are cleared,
   And the auctioneer wrings out his beard,
   And wipes his book, bedrenched and smeared,
And rakes the rain from his face with the edge of his hand,
   As torrents fall.

The wool of the ewes is like a sponge
　　With the daylong rain:
Jammed tight, to turn, or lie, or lunge,
　　They strive in vain.
Their horns are soft as finger-nails,
Their shepherds reek against the rails,
The tied dogs soak with tucked-in tails,
The buyers' hat-brims fill like pails,
Which spill small cascades when they shift their stand
　　In the daylong rain.

POSTSCRIPT

Time has trailed lengthily since met
　　At Pummery Fair
Those panting thousands in their wet
　　And woolly wear:
And every flock long since has bled,
And all the dripping buyers have sped,
And the hoarse auctioneer is dead,
Who 'Going-going!' so often said,
As he consigned to doom each meek, mewed band
　　At Pummery Fair.

Meeting at Night

ROBERT BROWNING

The gray sea and the long black land;
And the yellow half-moon large and low;
And the startled little waves that leap
In fiery ringlets from their sleep,
As I gain the cove with pushing prow,
And quench its speed in the slushy sand.

Then a mile of warm sea-scented beach;
Three fields to cross till a farm appears;
A tap at the pane, the quick sharp scratch
And blue spurt of a lighted match,
And a voice less loud, thro' its joys and fears,
Than the two hearts beating each to each.

My Lady's Grave

EMILY BRONTË

The linnet in the rocky dells,
   The moor-lark in the air,
The bee among the heather bells
   That hide my lady fair:

The wild deer browse above her breast;
   The wild birds raise their brood;
And they, her smiles of love caress'd,
   Have left her solitude!

I ween that when the grave's dark wall
   Did first her form retain,
They thought their hearts could ne'er recall
   The light of joy again.

They thought the tide of grief would flow
   Uncheck'd through future years;
But where is all their anguish now?
   And where are all their tears?

Well, let them fight for honour's breath,
   Or pleasure's shade pursue—
The dweller in the land of death
   Is changed and careless too.

And if their eyes should watch and weep
    Till sorrow's source were dry,
She would not, in her tranquil sleep,
    Return a single sigh?

Blow, west wind, by the lonely mound:
    And murmur, summer streams!
There is no need of other sound
    To soothe my lady's dreams.

The Lowest Trees have Tops

ATTRIBUTED TO SIR EDWARD DYER

The lowest trees have tops, the Ant her goal,
The flie her spleen, the little spark his heat,
And slender hairs cast shadows though but small,
And Bees have stings although they be not great.
Seas have their source, and so have shallow springs,
And love is love in beggars and in kings.

Where waters smoothest run, deep are the fordes,
The dial stires, yet none perceives it move:
The firmest faith is in the fewest words,
The Turtles cannot sing, and yet they love,
True hearts have eyes and ears, no tongues to speak
They hear, and see, and sigh, and then they break.

The Pigs and the Charcoal Burner

WALTER DE LA MARE

The old Pig said to the little pigs,
  'In the forest is truffles and mast,
Follow me then, all ye little pigs,
  Follow me fast!'

The Charcoal-burner sat in the shade,
  His chin on his thumb,
And saw the big Pig and the little pigs,
  Chuffling come.

He watched 'neath a green and giant bough,
  And the pigs in the ground
Made a wonderful grisling and gruzzling
  And greedy sound.

And when, full-fed, they were gone, and Night
  Walked her starry ways,
He stared with his cheeks in his hands
  At his sullen blaze.

The Ballad of Chevy Chase

ANONYMOUS

First Fit

The Percy out of Northumberland,
  And a vow to God made he
That he would hunt in the mountains
  Of Cheviat within days three,
In spite of the doughty Douglas
  And all that ever with him be.

The fattest harts in all Cheviat
   He said he would kill, and carry them away:
By my faith, said the doughty Douglas again,
   I will stop that hunting if that I may.

Then the Percy out of Banborough came,
   And with him a mighty company;
With fifteen hundred archers bold—
   They were chosen out of shires three.

This began on a Monday at morn
   In Cheviat the hills so high:
The child may rue that is unborn,
   It was the more pity.

The beaters through the woods went
   For to raise the deer;
Bowmen shot up on the slopes
   With their broad arrows clear.

Then the wild things through woods went
   On every side sheer;
Grey-hounds through the grooves glent
   For to kill their deer.

They began in Cheviat the hills above
   Early on a Monday:
By the time it drew to the hour of noon
   A hundred fat harts dead there lay.

They blew a 'kill' upon the bank
   They assembled on slopes sheer;
To the quarry then the Percy went
   To see the dressing of the deer.

He said, It was the Douglas's promise
   This day to meet me here;
But I knew he would fail, indeed:
   And a great oath the Percy swore.

At the last a Squire of Northumberland
   Looked at hand full nigh,
And was aware of the doughty Douglas coming:
   With him a great company.

Both with spear, billhook and blade:
   It was a mighty sight to see
Hardier men both of heart and hand
   Were not in Christianity.

They were twenty hundred spearmen good
   Without any fail;
They were coming along by the water of Tweed
   In the bounds of Tividale.

Leave off the dressing of the deer, he said
   And to your bows look you take good heed
For never since you were of your mother born
   Had ye never so much need.

The doughty Douglas on a steed
   He rode at his men before
His armour glittered as did a fire
   A bolder man was never born.

Tell me what men you are, he says
   Or whose men that you be:
Who gave you leave to hunt in this
   Cheviat Chase in spite of me?

The first man that ever him an answer made
    It was the good Lord Percy:
We will not tell you what men we are, he says
    Nor whose men that we be;
But we will hunt here in this Chase
    In the spite of thine, and of thee.

The fattest harts in all Cheviat
    We have killed, and cast to carry them away.
By my troth, said the doughty Douglas then,
    Therefore one of us shall die this day.

Then said the doughty Douglas
    Unto the Lord Percy:
To kill all these guiltless men,
    Alas! It were great pity.

But Percy, thou art a lord of land,
    I am an Earl called within my country:
Let all our men upon a party stand;
    And do the battle of you and of me.

Now Christ's corpse on his crown, says the Lord Percy,
    Whosoever thereto says nay.
By my troth, doughty Douglas, he says,
    Thou shalt never see that day;

Neither in England, Scotland, nor France,
    Nor for no man of a woman born,
But, and fortune be my chance,
    I dare meet him one man for one.

Then bespoke a squire of Northumberland
    Richard Witharington was his name;
It shall never be told in South England, he says,
    To King Henry the Fourth for shame.

I know you be great lords both,
    I am a poor squire of land;
I will never see any captain fight on a field
    And stand by myself, and look on,
And as long as I may my weapon wield
    I will not fail either heart or hand.

That day, that day, that dreadful day:
    The first fit here I find.
And if you will hear any more of the hunting at the Cheviat
    Yet is there more behind.

Second Fit

The English men had their bows y-bent
    Their hearts were good enough,
The first arrows that they shot off
    Seven score spearmen they slew.

Yet bides the Earl Douglas upon the bank
    A captain good enough
And that was seen truly
    For he wrought them both woe and harm.

The Douglas parted his host in three,
    Like a chief chieftain of pride,
With sure spears of mighty tree
    They come in on either side.

Through our English archery
    Gave many a wound full wide
Many a doughty man they made to die
    Which gained them no pride.

The English men let their bows be
    And pulled out blades that were bright:
It was a heavy sight to see
    Bright swords on basinets light.

Through rich mail and manoplie
  Many stern men they struck down straight;
Many a fellow that was full free
  They under foot did lay.

At last the Douglas and the Percy met
  Like two captains of might and main;
They swapped together till they both sweat
  With swords, that were of fine Milan.

These worthy fellows for to fight
  Thereto they were full keen
Till the blood out of their basinets sprent
  As ever did hail or rain.

Hold thee, Percy, said the Douglas,
  And in faith I shall thee bring,
Where thou shalt have an Earl's wages
  Of Jamie our Scottish king.

Thou shalt have thy ransom free
  I promise thee here this thing,
For the manfullest man yet art thou,
  That ever I conquered in field fighting.

Nay then, said the Lord Percy
  I told it thee before,
That I would never yielded be
  To no man of a woman born.

With that there came an arrow hastily
  Forth from a mighty man:
It hath stricken the Earl Douglas
  In at the breast bone.

Through liver and lungs both
　　The sharp arrow is gone
So that never after in all his life days
　　He spake no mae words but one,
That was, Fight ye my merry men, while you may,
　　For my life days are gone.

The Percy leaned on his blade
　　And saw the Douglas die:
He took the dead man by the hand
　　And said, woe is me for thee!

To have saved thy life I would have parted with
　　My lands for years three,
For a better man of heart nor of hand
　　Was not in all the north country.

Of all that power a Scottish knight
　　Was called Sir Hugh the Mongonbury.
He saw the Douglas to the death was dight
　　He took a spear, a trusty tree.

He rode upon a corsaire
　　Through a hundredth archery;
He never stinted, nor never reined
　　Till he came to the good lord Percy.

He set upon the lord Percy
　　A dint that was full sore:
With a sure spear of a mighty tree
　　Clean through the body he the Percy bore,

Out the other side, that a man might see
　　A large cloth-yard and more:
Two better captains were not in Christianity
　　Than that day slain were there.

An archer of Northumberland
   Saw slain was the lord Percy
He bore a bend-bow in his hand
   Was made of trusty tree.

An arrow, that a yard was long
   To the hard steel wound he:
A dint, that was both sad and sore
   He set on Sir Hugh the Mongonbury.

The dint it was both sad and sore
   That he on Mongonbury set
The swan feathers that his arrow bore
   With his heart blood they were wet.

There was no man there whose foot would flee
   But still in fight did stand,
Hewing on each other, while they could stand,
   With many a baleful blade.

This battle began in Cheviat
   An hour before the noon
And when the evensong bell was rung
   The battle was not half done.

They took on one on either hand
   By the light of the moon;
Many had no strength for to stand
   In Cheviat the hills among.

Of fifteen hundred archers of England
   Went away but fifty three
Of twenty hundred spearmen of Scotland
   But even five and fifty.

But all were slain Cheviat within:
  They had no strength to stand on high:
The child may rue that is unborn,
  It was the more pity.

There was slain with the lord Percy
  Sir John of Agerston,
Sir Roger the kind Hartly,
  Sir William the bold Hearon.
Sir George the worthy Lovel,
  A knight of great renown,
Sir Ralph the rich Rugby
  With dints were beaten down.

For Wetherington my heart was woe,
  That ever he slain should be;
For when his legs were hewn in two
  Yet he kneeled and fought on his knee.

There was slain with the doughty Douglas
  Sir Hugh the Mongonbury,
Sir Davy Londale, that worthy was,
  His sister's son was he:

Sir Charles Murray, in that place
  That never a foot would flee;
Sir Hugh Maxwell, a lord he was
  With the Douglas did he die.

So on the morrow they made them biers
  Of birch and hazell so gray,
Many widows with weeping tears
  Came to fetch their mates away.

Tividale may groan with grief
  Northumberland may make great moan,
For two such captains as slain were there
  In the march party shall never be known.

131

Word is come to Edinburgh
  To Jamie the Scottish king
That doughty Douglas, life-tenant of the Marches,
  He lay slain Cheviat within.

His hands did he clench and wring
  He said, Alas, and woe is me!
Such another captain Scotland within
  He said, in faith, should never be.

Word is come to lovely London
  To the fourth Harry our king,
That lord Percy, life-tenant of the Marches,
  He lay slain Cheviat within.

God have mercy on his soul, said King Harry,
  Good Lord, if thy will it be!
I have a hundred captains in England, he said
  As good as ever was he:
But Percy, if I keep my life,
  Thy death well quit shall be.

As our noble king made his vow
  Like a noble prince of renown;
For the death of the lord Percy
  He did the battle of Humbledon.

When six and thirty Scottish knights
  On a day were beaten down:
Glendale glittered on their armour bright
  Over castle, tower, and town.

This was the hunting of the Cheviat
  That rift began this spurn:
Old men that know the ground well enough
  Call it the Battle of Otterburn.

At Otterburn began this spurn
    Upon a Monday;
There was the doughty Douglas slain,
    The Percy never went away.

There was never a time on the march parties
    Since the Douglas and the Percy met,
But it was a marvel if the red blood ran not
    As the rain does in the street.

Jesu Christ our bales beat
    And to the bliss us bring:
This was the hunting of the Cheviat
    God send us all good ending!

Sir John Barleycorn

ANONYMOUS

There came three men from out of the west
Their victory to try;
And they have ta'en a solemn oath,
Poor Barleycorn should die.

They took a plough and ploughed him in,
Clods harrowed on his head;
And then they took a solemn oath
John Barleycorn was dead.

There he lay sleeping in the ground
Till rain did on him fall;
Then Barleycorn sprung up his head,
And so amazed them all.

There he remained till Midsummer
And look'd both pale and wan;
Then Barleycorn he got a beard
And so became a man.

Then they sent men with scythes so sharp
To cut him off at knee;
And then poor Johnny Barleycorn
They served most barbarouslie.

Then they sent men with pitchforks strong
To pierce him through the heart;
And like a doleful Tragedy
They bound him in a cart.

And then they brought him to a barn
A prisoner to endure;
And so they fetched him out again,
And laid him on the floor.

Then they set men with holly clubs,
To beat the flesh from th' bones;
But the miller served him worse than that,
He ground him 'twixt two stones.

O! Barleycorn is the choicest grain
That e'er was sown on land:
It will do more than any grain
By the turning of your hand.

It will make a boy into a man,
A man into an ass:
To silver it will change your gold,
Your silver into brass.

It will make the huntsman hunt the fox,
That never wound a horn;
It will bring the tinker to the stocks
That people may him scorn.

O! Barleycorn is the choicest grain
That e'er was sown on land.
And it will cause a man to drink
Till he neither can go nor stand.

Calm after Storm (from 'Resolution and Independence')

WILLIAM WORDSWORTH

There was a roaring in the wind all night;
The rain came heavily and fell in floods;
But now the sun is rising calm and bright;
The birds are singing in the distant woods;
Over his own sweet voice the Stock-dove broods;
The Jay makes answer as the Magpie chatters;
And all the air is filled with pleasant noise of waters.

All things that love the sun are out of doors;
The sky rejoices in the morning's birth;
The grass is bright with rain-drops;—on the moors
The hare is running races in her mirth;
And with her feet from the plashy earth
Raises a mist; that, glittering in the sun,
Runs with her all the way, wherever she doth run.

Birds' Nests

EDWARD THOMAS

The summer nests uncovered by autumn wind,
Some torn, others dislodged, all dark,
Everyone sees them: low or high in tree,
Or hedge, or single bush, they hang like a mark.

Since there's no need of eyes to see them with
I cannot help a little shame
That I missed most, even at eye's level, till
The leaves blew off and made the seeing no game.

'Tis a light pang. I like to see the nests
Still in their places, now first known,
At home and by far roads. Boys knew them not,
Whatever jays and squirrels may have done.

And most I like the winter nests deep-hid
That leaves and berries fell into:
Once a dormouse dined there on hazel-nuts,
And grass and goose-grass seeds found soil and grew.

A Backward Spring

THOMAS HARDY

The trees are afraid to put forth buds,
And there is timidity in the grass;
The plots lie gray where gouged by spuds,
    And whether next week will pass
Free of sly sour winds is the fret of each bush
    Of barberry waiting to bloom.

Yet the snowdrop's face betrays no gloom,
And the primrose pants in its heedless push,
Though the myrtle asks if it's worth the fight
   This year with frost and rime
   To venture one more time
On delicate leaves and buttons of white
From the selfsame boughs as at last year's prime,
And never to ruminate on or remember
What happened to it in mid-December.

Dust of Snow

ROBERT FROST

The way a crow
Shook down on me
The dust of snow
From a hemlock tree

Has given my heart
A change of mood
And saved some part
Of a day I had rued.

A Lyke-Wake Dirge

ANONYMOUS

This ae nighte, this ae nighte,
  —*Every nighte and alle,*
Fire and fleet and candle-lighte,
  And Christe receive thy saule.

When thou from hence away art past,
—*Every nighte and alle,*
To Whinny-muir thou com'st at last:
And Christe receive thy saule.

If ever thou gavest hosen and shoon,
—*Every nighte and alle,*
Sit thee down and put them on:
And Christe receive thy saule.

If hosen and shoon thou ne'er gav'st nane
—*Every nighte and alle,*
The whinnes sall prick thee to the bare bane;
And Christe receive thy saule.

From Whinny-muir when thou may'st pass,
—*Every nighte and alle,*
To Brig o' Dread thou com'st at last;
And Christe receive thy saule.

From Brig o' Dread when thou may'st pass,
—*Every nighte and alle,*
To Purgatory fire thou com'st at last;
And Christe receive thy saule.

If ever thou gavest meat or drink,
—*Every nighte and alle,*
The fire sall never make thee shrink;
And Christe receive thy saule.

If meat or drink thou ne'er gav'st nane,
—*Every nighte and alle,*
The fire will burn thee to the bare bane;
And Christe receive thy saule.

This ae nighte, this ae nighte,
—*Every nighte and alle,*
Fire and fleet and candle-lighte,
And Christe receive thy saule.

Inversnaid

GERARD MANLEY HOPKINS

This darksome burn, horseback brown,
His rollrock highroad roaring down,
In coop and in comb the fleece of his foam
Flutes and low to the lake falls home.

A windpuff-bonnet of fáwn-fróth
Turns and twindles over the broth
Of a pool so pitchblack, féll-frówning,
It rounds and rounds Despair to drowning.

Degged with dew, dappled with dew
Are the groins of the braes that the brook treads through,
Wiry heathpacks, flitches of fern,
And the beadbonny ash that sits over the burn.

What would the world be, once bereft
Of wet and of wildness? Let them be left,
O let them be left, wildness and wet;
Long live the weeds and the wilderness yet.

Bushes and Briars

ANONYMOUS

Through bushes and through briars
I lately took my way,
All for to hear the small birds sing
And the lambs to skip and play.

I overheard my own true love
Her voice did sound so clear:
'Long time I have been waiting for
The coming of my dear.'

'Sometimes I am uneasy
And troubled in my mind
Sometimes I think I'll go to my love
And tell to him my mind.'

'But if I should go to my love
My love he will say "Nay";
If I show to him my boldness,
He'll ne'er love me again.'

Time and the Bell (from 'Burnt Norton')

T. S. ELIOT

Time and the bell have buried the day,
The black cloud carries the sun away.
Will the sunflower turn to us, will the clematis
Stray down, bend to us; tendril and spray
Clutch and cling?

Chill
Fingers of yew be curled
Down on us? after the kingfisher's wing
Has answered light to light, and is silent, the light is still
At the still point of the turning world.

Old Mother Laidinwool

RUDYARD KIPLING

'Twas all a warm September an' the hops had flourished grand,
She saw the folks get into 'em with stockin's on their hands;
An' none of 'em was foreigners but all which she had known,
And old Mother Laidinwool she blessed 'em every one.
She saw her daughters picking an' their children them-beside,
An' she moved among the babies an' she stilled 'em when
        they cried.
She saw their clothes was bought, not begged an' they was clean
        an' fat,
An' old Mother Laidinwool she thanked the Lord for that.

Cumulative Rhyme for Twelfth Night

ANONYMOUS

 Twelve huntsmen with horns and hounds
  Hunting over other men's grounds!

 Eleven ships sailing the main,
  Some bound for France and some for Spain;
 I wish them all safe home again.

 Ten comets in the sky,
  Some low and some high;

Nine peacocks in the air,
  I wonder how they all came there;
I do not know and I do not care.

Eight joiners in a joiners' hall,
  Working with the tools and all;

Seven lobsters in a dish,
  As fresh as any heart could wish;

Six beetles against the wall,
  Close by an old woman's apple stall;

Five puppies of our dog Ball,
  Who daily for their breakfast call;

Four horses stuck in a bog.
  Three monkeys tied to a clog;

Two pudding ends would choke a dog,
  With a gaping wide-mouthed waddling frog.

Words for a Madrigal

SIR WALTER RALEIGH

What is our life? A play of passion
Our mirth the music of division.
Our mothers' wombs the tiring houses be
Where we are dressed for this short comedy.
Heaven the judicious sharp spectator is
That sits and marks who still doth act amiss.
Our graves that hide us from the searching sun
Are like drawn curtains when the play is done;
Thus march we playing to our latest rest,
Only we die in earnest: that's no jest.

Missel Thrush

WALTER DE LA MARE

When from the brittle ice the fields
Begin to spring with green,
Then sits the storm-cock tree-top high,
And shrills the blasts between.

And when the sun, with thinning ray,
Tells winter's drawing nigh,
Still this wild bird, of valiant heart,
Shouts wild against the sky.

A Bird-Scene at a Rural Dwelling

THOMAS HARDY

When the inmate stirs, the birds retire discreetly
From the window-ledge, whereon they whistled sweetly
    And on the step of the door,
    In the misty morning hoar;
  But now the dweller is up they flee
  To the crooked neighbouring codlin-tree;
And when he comes fully forth they seek the garden,
And call from the lofty costard, as pleading pardon
    For shouting so near before
    In their joy at being alive:—
Meanwhile the hammering clock within goes five.

I know a domicile of brown and green,
Where for a hundred summers there have been
Just such enactments, just such daybreaks seen.

Where in a lusty plain (from The King's Quire)

JAMES I OF SCOTLAND

Where in a lusty plain took I my way
 Along a river, pleasant to behold,
Embroidered all with fresh flowers gay,
 Where through the gravel, bright as any gold,
The crystal water ran so clear and cold
 That in mine ear it made continually
A maner sound mingled with harmony.

That full of little fishes by the brim
 Now here now there, with backs as blue as lead
Did lap and play, and in a rout did swim
 So prettily, and dressed them to spread
Their coral fins, as is the ruby red
 That in the sun upon their scales bright
As glistening aye glittered in my sight.

And by this same riverside below
 A highway found I there like to been
On which, on every side, a long row
 Of trees saw I full of leaves green
That full of fruit delightful wereto seen
 And also, as it come unto my mind
Of beasts saw I many diverse kind:

The lion king and his fierce lioness;
 The panther like unto the smaragdine;
The little squirrel full of business;
 The slow ass, the drudging beast of pain;
The sly ape; the war-like porcupine;
 The piercing lynx; the lover unicorn,
That voids out venom from his ivory horn.

144

There saw I dress him, new out of his haunt,
  The fierce tiger, full of felony;
The dromedary; the stander elephant;
  The wily fox, the widow's enemy,
The gate-climber: the elk for alblastry;
  The hearkening boar; the wholesome greyhound dogs;
The hare also that oft goes into hortis;

The buffalo, drawer by his horns great;
  The sable martin, fawn, and many more;
The chalk white ermine, tipped with jet;
  The royal hart, the coney, and the roe;
The wolf, that of the murder says not no;
  The lusty beaver, and the ravening bear;
Chameleon; the camel full of hair.

With many another beast diverse and strange
  That cometh not just now into my mind...

Last Night

CHRISTINA ROSSETTI

Where were you last night? I watched at the gate;
I went down early, I stayed down late.
  Were you snug at home, I should like to know,
Or were you in the coppice wheedling Kate?

She's a fine girl, with a fine clear skin;
Easy to woo, perhaps not hard to win.
  Speak up like a man and tell me the truth:
I'm not one to grow downhearted and thin.

If you love her best, speak up like a man;
It's not I will stand in the light of your plan:
 Some girls might cry and scold you a bit,
And say they couldn't bear it; but I can.

Love was pleasant enough, and the days went fast;
Pleasant while it lasted, but it needn't last;
 Awhile on the wax, and awhile on the wane,
Now dropped away into the past.

Was it pleasant to you? to me it was:
Now clean gone as an image from glass,
 As a goodly rainbow that fades away,
As dew that steams upward from the grass;

As the first spring day or the last summer day,
As the sunset flush that leaves heaven grey,
 As a flame burnt out for lack of oil,
Which no pains relight or ever may.

Good luck to Kate and good luck to you:
I guess she'll be kind when you come to woo.
 I wish her a pretty face that will last,
I wish her a husband steady and true.

Hate you? not I, my very good friend;
All things begin and all have an end.
 But let broken be broken; I put no faith
In quacks who set up to patch and mend.

Just my love and one word to Kate—
Not to let time slip if she means to mate;
 For even such a thing has been known
As to miss the chance while we weigh and wait.

My Mary

JOHN CLARE

Who lives where beggars rarely speed,
And leads a hum-drum life indeed,
As none beside herself would lead?
           My Mary.

Who lives where noises never cease,
And what with hogs and ducks and geese
Can never have minute's peace?
           My Mary.

Who nearly battled to her chin,
Bangs down the yard through thick and thin,
Nor picks her road, nor cares a pin?
           My Mary.

Who, save in Sunday's bib and tuck,
Goes daily waddling like a duck,
O'er head and ears in grease and muck?
           My Mary.

Unus'd to pattens or to clogs,
Who takes the swill to serve the hogs,
And steals the milk for cats and dogs?
           My Mary.

Who, frost and snow, as hard as nails,
Stands out o' doors, and never fails
To wash up things and scour the pails?
           My Mary.

Who bustles night and day, in short,
At all catch jobs of every sort,
And gains her mistress' favour for't?
           My Mary.

And who is oft repaid with praise,
In doing what her mistress says,
And yielding to her whimmy ways?
   My Mary.

For her there's none apter, I believe,
At 'creeping up a mistress' sleeve',
Than this low kindred stump of Eve,
   My Mary.

Who when the baby's all unfit,
To please its mamma kisses it,
And vows no rose on earth's so sweet?
   My Mary.

But when her mistress is not nigh,
Who swears, and wishes it would die,
And pinches it and makes it cry?
   My Mary.

Oh, rank deceit! what soul could think—
But gently there, revealing ink:
At faults of thine thy friend must wink,
   My Mary.

Who, not without a 'spark o' pride',
Though strong as grunter's bristly hide,
Doth keep her hair in papers tied?
   My Mary.

And, mimicking the gentry's way,
Who strives to speak as fine as they,
And minds but every word they say?
   My Mary.

And who, though's well bid blind to see
As her to tell ye A from B,
Thinks herself none o' low degree?
    My Mary.

Who prates and runs o'er silly stuff,
And 'mong the boys makes sport enough,
So ugly, silly, droll and rough?
    My Mary.

Ugly! Muse, for shame of thee,
What faults art thou a-going to see
In one, that's 'lotted out to be
    My Mary?

Who low in stature, thick and fat,
Turns brown from going without a hat,
Though not a pin the worse for that?
    My Mary.

Who's laugh'd at too by every whelp,
For failings which she cannot help?
But silly fools will laugh and chelp,
    My Mary.

For though in stature mighty small,
And near as thick as thou art tall,
The hand made thee that made us all,
    My Mary.

And though thy nose hooks down too much,
And prophesies thy chin to touch,
I'm not so nice to look at such,
    My Mary.

No, no; about thy nose and chin,
It's hooking out, or bending in,
I never heed or care a pin,
   My Mary.

And though thy skin is brown and rough,
And form'd nature hard and tough,
All suiteth me! so that's enough,
   My Mary.

Winter Snowstorm

JOHN CLARE

Winter is come in earnest, and the snow,
In dazzling splendour crumping underfoot,
Spreads a white world all calm, and where we go
By hedge or wood trees shine from top to root
In feathered foliage, flashing light and shade
In strangest contrast; fancy's pliant eye
Delighted sees a vast romance displayed
And fairy halls descended from the sky;
The smallest twig its snowy burthen bears,
And woods o'erhead the dullest eyes engage
To shape strange things where arch and pillar bears
A roof of grains fantastic, arched, and high;
A little shed beside the spinney wears
The grotesque semblance of an hermitage.

Jesse James

ANONYMOUS

Yes, I went down to the depot
  Not many days ago: they followed on behind,
And I fell upon my knees, and I offered up the keys
  To Frank and his brother, Jesse James.

Poor Jesse James, poor Jesse James,
  He robbed that Danville train;
Yes, the dirty little coward, he shot Mr. Howard,
  An' they laid poor Jesse in his grave.

Frank says to Jesse, not many days ago,
  'Lets rob that Danville train.'
An' Jesse says to Frank, 'We'll take it as we go,
  For we may not be hyer any more.'

Jesse was a man, an' he travelled over the land,
  With his sword an' his pistol to his side.
Robert Ford watched his eye an' shot him on the sly,
  An' they laid poor Jesse James in his grave.

Yes, Jesse had a wife, the darlin' of his life,
  An' the children all was brave.
Robert Ford watched his eye an' shot him on the sly.
  An' they laid poor Jesse in his grave.

It was on Friday night, the moon was shinin' bright,
  An' Jesse was standin' 'fore his glass,
Robert Ford's pistol ball brought him tremblin' from the wall,
  An' they laid poor Jesse in his grave.

Well, the people of the West, when they heard of Jesse's death,
    They wondered how he come to die.
Robert Ford watched his eye an' shot him on the sly,
    An' they laid poor Jesse in his grave.

Poor Jesse James, poor Jesse James,
    He robbed that Danville train;
Yes, the dirty little coward, he shot Mr. Howard,
    An' they laid poor Jesse in his grave.

ACKNOWLEDGEMENTS

For permission to reproduce copyright material, acknowledgement is made to the following:

Arthur Waley and Messrs Constable and Company Limited ('The Pedlar of Spells', 'Lament of Hsi-Chun', 'The Little Cart', 'The Red Cockatoo', 'Releasing a Migrant Yen or Wild Goose' from 170 Chinese Poems); Arthur Waley and Messrs Allen and Unwin ('Chinese Song of Courtship', 'Return from Battle' from Chinese Poems); the Literary Trustees of Walter de la Mare and the Society of Authors as their representative Messrs Faber and Faber ('A Widow's Weeds', 'Thunder', 'Miss T.', 'Tillie', 'The Pool in the Rock', 'The Orchard', 'The Pigs and the Charcoal Burner', 'Missel Thrush'); the Trustees of the Hardy Estate and Messrs Macmillan and Company Limited ('Birds at Winter Nightfall', 'The House of Hospitalities', 'If it's ever spring again', 'Last week in October', 'A Sheep Fair', 'A Backward Spring', 'A Bird Scene at a Rural Dwelling', from Collected Poems and 'In a Wood' from The Woodlanders); The Bodley Head ('Winter Warfare', 'A Glimpse into the Great Beyond' from Collected Poems by Edgell Rickword); Mrs Edward Thomas and Messrs Faber and Faber ('Thaw', 'Tall Nettles', 'A Tale', 'Digging', 'The Owl', 'Woods', 'A Cat', 'Birds' Nests'); Messrs Faber and Faber ('New Hampshire', and 'Time and the Bell' from Burnt Norton by T. S. Eliot); Mrs W. B. Yeats and Messrs Macmillan ('Down by the Salley Gardens', 'The Song of the Old Mother', 'The Song of Wandering Aengus', 'The Cat and the Moon' from Collected Poems of W. B. Yeats); Messrs Angus and Robertson Limited ('Frying Pan's Theology', 'A Bushman's Song' by A. B. Paterson); Mr Robert Graves and Messrs Cassell and Company Limited ('Love without Hope' from Collected Poems, 1959); Messrs Jonathan Cape Limited and Messrs Henry Holt and Company Incorporated ('Stopping by woods on a Snowy Evening', 'Dust of Snow' from the complete works of Robert Frost); Messrs Chatto and Windus ('Marching' by Isaac Rosenburg); Mrs G. Bambridge and Messrs Macmillan and Company Limited ('Old Mother Laidinwool' from Puck of Pook's Hill by Rudyard Kipling); Oxford University Press ('Hailstorm in May', 'Pied Beauty' from Poems of Gerard Manley Hopkins); Miss Maud Karpeles and Oxford University Press ('The Derby Ram', 'The Shad', 'Good Old Man',

'Sourwood Mountain', 'Lady Isabel and the Elf Knight', 'Springfield Mountain' from English Folksongs from the Southern Appalachians, Collector/Arranger Cecil J. Sharp); Novello and Company Limited ('Dance to your Daddy', 'Lady Maisry', 'Three Little Tailors', 'Cocky Robin', 'Edward', 'Nottamun Town', 'The Ground Hog', 'The Cuckoo', 'Sir John Barleycorn', 'Bushes and Briars', Collector/Arranger Cecil J. Sharp); Messrs Angus and Robertson Limited ('The Crows Kept Flyin' Up' from Old Bush Songs collected by Douglas Stewart and Nancy Keesing); Messrs William Heinemann ('If All the World were Paper', 'The Heron' from English and Scottish Ballads, edited by Robert Graves); Messrs Harper Brothers ('The Flying Cloud', 'Lovewell's Flight', The Gold Vanity', 'The Bitter Withy', 'The Avondale Mine Disaster', 'Jesse James' from the Ballad Book, edited by MacEdward Leach); A. L. Lloyd ('A Little Boy Threw', 'The Big Rock Candy Mountains', 'The Bullwhacker', 'John Hardy' from Corn on the Cob); A. L. Lloyd and Messrs Lawrence and Wishart Limited ('Cushie Butterfield' (rewritten by David Holbrook) and 'The Sandgate Girl's Lamentation' from Come All Ye Bold Miners); Curwen Edition ('Hanging Johnny'); The Folk-Lore Society ('Tarra Ding Ding Ding Dido', 'Game Rhyme' from The Games and Diversions of Argyllshire). For two of the verses of the folksong 'The Cuckoo' acknowledgement is made to James Reeves (The Idiom of the People) and Messrs Heinemann.

INDEX OF AUTHORS

The references are to pages

155